Buy
Your Own
MARKY MARKETTE!

W9-BRD-510

BE REMARKABLE!
BEST,
EK

Praise for Reality Marketing Revolution

"If you are one of thousands of business owners struggling to fulfill your dream of entrepreneurialism—read this book now."

> - Jeffrey Fox, author of "*How To Become A Rainmaker*"

"We're big fans of Reality Marketing and have seen first hand how these ideas can revolutionize any small business and put it on the fast track to explosive growth and prosperity. This is a wake up call to entrepreneurs around the world: join Mike and Eric's revolution and take control of your marketing, business and lives."

> - Jimmy Vee & Travis Miller, authors of "*Gravitational Marketing: The Science of Attracting Customers*" and founders of GravitationalMarketing.com

"This book is full of useful and valuable information on how to market way smarter and have your dollars work way better. Not just a book, but a workbook for the entrepreneur who wants to out-market the competition."

> - Chet Holmes, author of the #1 business book, "*The Ultimate Sales Machine*"

"Finally! A book filled with real-life innovative marketing ideas that will help any small business owner generate more leads and keep their pipeline full."

> - Gene Marks, author, "*The Streetwise Small Business Book of Lists*"

"Reality Marketing...is a terrific overview, especially for small businesses with limited budgets. The authors really capture the common mistakes and show how better to optimize time and money for real marketing results."

- Amie J. Devero, author of "*Powered by Principle*"

"Reality Marketing grabs your hand and leads you through everything you need to know and do to dramatically increase your revenues and profitability. A graduate degree in effective marketing concentrated into an easy to read book filled with practical advice that you can start to use immediately to pump up your sales."

- Steven Smolinsky, author "*Conversation On Networking*" and Project Faculty at The Wharton School, University of Pennsylvania, Speaker and Consultant.

"Reality Marketing provides small businesses with exactly what they need: A no nonsense approach to improving sales, profitability and for building long-term customer relationships! I loved it!"

- Eyal Maoz, Visiting Assistant Professor of Marketing, Kellogg School of Management

"The energy in which Eric and Mike communicate in person is amplified in Reality Marketing Revolution. Their passion to support and provide guidance to entrepreneurs and small business owners is clearly stated in a step by step format in this book. You will walk away with many creative ideas and approaches that will allow you to crystallize a clear marketing direction that will provide increased revenue and profits while reducing expenses— a win win for all! "

- Joan Walsh author "*Ready, Set, Plan, Go!*" and a founding partner in the consulting firm FSMI

Reality Marketing
Revolution

Transform Your Small Business into a Money Making Machine!

Mike Lieberman & Eric Keiles

A LINX Book

Books are available for special promotions and premiums. For details,
contact Special Markets, LINX, Corp., Box 613, Great Falls, VA
22066, or e-mail specialmarkets@linxcorp.com.

Printed in the United States of America

Book cover design by Katie Dunford and Justin Phillips of Square 2
Marketing and Paul Fitzgerald

Interior book design by Paul Fitzgerald

Edited by Sandra Gurvis

ISBN 0-9802118-2-4

Dedication:

We dedicate our first book to all the entrepreneurs
who took the leap of faith to start their
own businesses and live the life they've
always dreamed.

We also want to thank the incredible team at
Square 2 Marketing for tirelessly helping those
entrepreneurs achieve their dreams.

▌Table of Contents

Foreword

A revolution occurs when a majority of people challenge a common belief they have been told to accept as true. During the American Revolution, the new thinking was that our country should be free from the tyranny of the British Empire so our citizens could pursue their personal goals and dreams.

For decades, business owners, entrepreneurs, and marketers followed the advice of traditional ad agencies. But mass advertising like radio, TV, and billboards no longer fit the new reality. So it's time for a Reality Marketing ™ revolution – to create new models of marketing that will better promote your small business; to "rage against the machine" that has taught business people like yourself to implement marketing programs in an outdated fashion.

In Reality Marketing™, we offer new marketing strategies and tactics that will realistically meet the budgets and goals of small business owners. We'll show you how to slash your expenses and increase the response to your marketing, all the while generating more business opportunities and accelerating growth.

My partner, Mike Lieberman, and I felt the pressing need to write this book so we could pass along our knowledge and methods to the business world. Previously?, the information was only available to our clients and prospects. However, we wanted to expand the "revolution" and share how you can think about marketing in a different manner by following basic steps. Then you can live the life you've always wanted, seeing a profit from your business, and reaping the work-life balance that can make entrepreneurship so rewarding.

We only ask one thing. In a revolution, one person tells another until the new ideology sweeps the community. If you feel the Reality Marketing™ methodology is valuable enough for you to change your thinking, pass it on to a friend who owns a business and see if you can help them also achieve their dreams.

For more information, check out realitymarketingrevolution.com. And the best of luck in all your marketing endeavors!

Eric Keiles,
Chief Marketing Officer
Square 2 Marketing

▌▌Chapter 1
IS THIS YOU?

When we ask our prospects, "Tell us about your company," invariably their reply is something like, "We have good service and a great staff and neat products and lots of great things going on." Their struggle occurs when they try to share this information with the world. They try to execute marketing tactics like advertising but get frustrated when the results don't materialize. Figure 1.1 shows how marketing messages are rebuffed by a gray amorphous cloud called "market noise."

Your Company   *Your Prospects*

Figure 1.1

What, exactly, is market noise? It could be one of several things:
- Your competition is yelling louder.
- You're saying the right things to the wrong people.
- You are saying the wrong thing to the right people.
- Your clients are too busy to hear your message.
- You are sending the messages in the wrong medium.

Our job as small business owners, entrepreneurs, and marketers is to build a bridge over the market noise, to get to the prospects. Figure 1.2 shows how some prospects Note: the dashes should match – the ones with the dollar signs – are ready to buy now, while those with the question marks are interested in your service, but maybe not today. We'll show you in Chapter 11 how to build a prospect database.

Inside Excellence vs. Outside Perception

Figure 1.2

Your job is also to make sure your company's inside excellence translates into messages for the outside world. This ensures that prospects' and clients' perception of you is equal to the good things you are doing now.   All the while, you are building a case as to why you are the obvious choice to do business with.

Here's an example.   We were approached by a custom home construction company that was expanding its services to renovating kitchens and bathrooms in older homes. The owner came to us needing a print campaign to advertise his business . He wanted us to just design the new ads.

No problem. We asked him the same five questions that we pose to every prospect:

What are the company's revenue goals over the next 12-18 months?

Who is the exact target audience that will purchase your service?

What pains and problems does this target market have when they purchase services like yours?

What solutions does your company provide to cure those pains?

How are those solutions remarkable enough to start a buzz and set you apart from the competition?

These simple questions are what make up a basic marketing strategy statement. When we put them to the builder, he immediately realized he hadn't effectively planned to execute any marketing programs—he was just jumping right to the tactics. Heck, he didn't even have a name for the new service and he was already worried about the ads! **Strategy before tactics is a must when it comes to crafting an effective marketing effort.**

Strategy before tactics...but what does that mean, exactly?It's common for people to feel pressure to jump right in and start with marketing tactics. "Build me a Website," they say. "I want to start some newspaper advertising. We need a new PowerPoint presentation." But these tactics need to be organized and integrated into an overall plan or strategy. That way, the efforts put forth to create an effective strategy will insure that the tactics get results in line with the company's overall goals.

We have seen too many marketing dollars wasted on tactics without any connection to an overall strategy or plan. That is why we insist on *strategy before tactics* with every client and assignment. Our job is also to ensure that tactics like advertising are part of a larger plan with goals, objectives, and metrics to effectively measure their success.

Here's another example. The owner of a local restaurant decided to retire. The location was fantastic, so a successful entrepreneur in the construction industry leased the spot and decided to open a new hamburger café, a venture he'd never tried before. He called us, looking for help with his Website. Again, we asked the five questions and his only answer was, "We're going to use fresh ground beef, not frozen."

What? That's all you've got? That's going to be the reason people line up to sample your fare, tell all their friends, make plans to meet there, and spend lots of money for years to come?

We can only say, as we did to him, that his fate was sealed. Just like opening up the "greatest retail store on the North Pole" is futile, having a business without a basic marketing strategy spells certain death.

 **Reality Byte**

Small Business Success

Three things you need:

1. The ability to abandon a plan when it doesn't work
2. The confidence to do the right thing even when it costs you money in the short run
3. Enough belief in other people that you don't try to do everything yourself.

Seth Godin
Author and Blogger
www.sethgodin.com

Unfortunately, most small- and medium- sized business owners cannot answer the five questions. Often they are exceptional tacticians—expert at what they do for a living as manufacturers, lawyers, doctors, insurance brokers, home builders, or restaurateurs – but, because they lack training in marketing, they are unable to figure out how to create an effective marketing strategy or plan.

When asked those five questions, most fall back on generic answers like, "We want to get our name out there," or "We're going to use fresh instead of frozen hamburger meat."

Don't be that person. Don't get caught being ordinary and unremarkable. Read the following chapters and change the way you market your company.

Each chapter will end with tips to get you started. If you execute these simple tips you will see instant improvements in your marketing.

Start Today! Tips

1. Set aside a 30-minute period each week for reviewing past marketing activities and making future plans. Do this on a week-by-week basis, chronicling your activities and charting your progress (or lack thereof)

2. Create a projected revenue figure for your company for the next 6 or 12 months.

3. Calculate how much additional revenue you have to produce to hit these goals.

4. Estimate a marketing budget you would be comfortable spending to achieve the new level of sales.

▎Chapter 2

WHY THE OLD MARKETING SYSTEM IS BROKEN

"Please, please, please…let this one work…"

Sound familiar? You have plenty of company if you find yourself thinking this every time you launch a new marketing or advertising campaign. While many small- to medium-size enterprises do a pretty good job of producing a product or providing a service, they struggle mightily when it comes to promoting their business.

We see it time and time again in our work as marketing professionals. Beautifully designed newspaper ads are ignored. Direct mailers end up in the trash. Seemingly well-placed billboards fail to grab the drivers' attention (perhaps a good thing, especially in heavy traffic). Radio and TV ads annoy rather than engage or are muted, flipped to a new channel, or fast-forwarded using a DVR.

Nothing seems to work. Yet you're putting forth all this time and money to promote your business. "What am I doing wrong?" you might ask.

Before you start feeling bad about yourself and your company, understand it's not entirely your fault. You can turn things around and create marketing strategies that get you noticed and drive customers to your door– rather than away from it. But only if you change the way you think about marketing your company.

You need to forget everything you've ever learned about marketing and advertising. Most likely, you're working under the old system – one that is broken and about as obsolete as a slide rule.

Not long ago, promoting your business or product was relatively easy. Consider the example of breakfast cereal. Prior to the 1940s, the most common breakfast was bacon and eggs. Every morning, families across America would wake up early and start cooking. Then the Kellogg brothers invented Corn Flakes. This radically changed the way people thought about their morning meal – just open a box and pour it into a bowl! As the word spread, about this new breakfast option, consumers visited grocery stores to search for this new product. When they discovered the new "cereal section" in the store, there was only one choice—corn flakes.

Not only were there few competitors, there was only one *kind* of corn flakes – plain. This was how most of the world was back then. It's like Henry Ford's famous quote about the Model T; customers can have "any color they want as long as it's black." You had limited choices back then and, generally speaking, customers were OK with that. Who knew anything else?

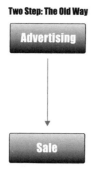

Figure 2.1

As late as the 1970s, there were only three TV networks, a fairly small number of radio and newspaper outlets and no Internet. So it was relatively easy to promote and sell a product like corn flakes. You advertised in the few media outlets available, put it on the shelves and sold the item or service. It's what we call "two-step marketing," illustrated in Figure 2.1 – you advertise, customers buy.

Today, all you have to do is visit your local supermarket to see how dramatically things have changed. There are now well over 50 different kinds of cereals on the shelves, with dozens of corn flake variations alone – plain, sugar-coated, vitamin-fortified, with berries, with nuts...the list goes on and on. Plus, add in all of the breakfast bars (including those made with corn flake variants), instant oatmeal, microwave egg and cheese sandwiches and it turns into a marketing nightmare!

So take your product and magnify it a thousand fold. Nearly everything you can think of has been duplicated, tweaked, or repackaged ten times over. Remember when there used to be one Coke or only one place in town to get your car fixed? Now there are dozens.

Not only are there myriad products and services, but you have an infinite number of places and ways to promote them. In addition to hundreds of TV channels, and millions of Websites, there are newspapers (including neighborhood and "alternative" publications), magazines, movie screens, direct mailers, coupon books, buses, billboards, blimps, e-mail, cell phones, PDAs, RSS feeds, and blogs. Even the backs of bathroom stalls and celebrities can be used to market your company these days.

Advertising and marketing have splintered into a million different niches and become so cluttered that it is getting increasingly difficult to stand out. According to a 2001 white paper published by the consulting firm, Accenture, most Americans are exposed to an average of 3,000 advertisements a day. No wonder we are so numb to traditional advertising.

Long gone are the days when people bought your product or service simply because you made it available –put it on a shelf, so to speak. It's no longer enough to present your product or service to the public and expect it to sell. Now, the *public* selects what *it* wants. It's a great paradigm shift for the consumer but nothing but trouble for business owners like us.

Thus, the old system of "two-step marketing" – you advertise and customers buy – is broken. Today, we live in a world of "three-step marketing; " one that involves the use of new strategies to vault over, sneak under, or cut through the advertising/marketing noise so you can sell your product or service. In this diagram, we show the extra step in building a prospect database (more on this in Chapter 11 and 12).

Figure 2.2

The problem is, not many small- and medium- sized business owners know how to effectively do this, so they continue to try the same old things. They take out hugely expensive billboards or place ineffective ads in the local newspapers, radio, or cable TV. They copy big company marketing tactics – large brands with completely different goals and objectives – with the feckless hope that they can duplicate their success. This approach can work if they have "unlimited" advertising budgets like the big players. But we have yet to meet a small business client with that kind of budget.

So it's just not going to work for entrepreneurs today. In this not-so-brave new world of marketing, if you want your business to succeed, you need to give people a *reason* to buy or use your product or service, one that makes it stand out from all the rest. You'll find out more about this in upcoming chapters.

By now, you may be saying to yourself, "OK, I see that the old system is broken. But what am I supposed to do?"

Read on…. But first, attack these Start Today Tips.

Start Today! Tips

1. List all the marketing activities you spent money on during the last 12 months, everything from Yellow Page ads to Website banners to signage to fliers and more.

2. Review these activities and identify those that generated results and those that did not.

3. Review your internal database for prospect information and make sure you can capture key components like "referral source" and e-mail address.

4. Answer these key questions:
   a. How many prospects are in your prospect database? ____
   b. How many e-mail addresses do you have? ____
   c. How many mailing addresses do you have? ____
   d. Who is responsible for collecting prospect contact information at your company? _____

▌Chapter 3
REALITY MARKETING™

Does this sound familiar? You've put your marketing plans into place, your advertisements are running and you're sitting back waiting for all of the customers to flock to your door. Still not working you say?

Instead of reworking your advertisements, you probably want to rethink the *message* you are using in your ads and reset what you expect to happen as a result of the ads.

That's the basis for what we call Reality Marketing™ and it's the best way to ensure pinpoint delivery of your messages directly to your target market. The result is a more direct way through all that market noise we talked about in the first chapter.

Never heard of Reality Marketing™? That's because it's a new way to approach the task of marketing your company – no matter what your industry, product, size or revenue.

The essence of Reality Marketing™ involves identifying your customers' "pains" – the problems, challenges, issues or hurdles they face in relation to your product or service.

For example, if you own a retail dry cleaning business one of your customers' pains is the hassle of having to drive to your store to drop off and pick up clothes. Or, if you own a restaurant, a long wait for a table when you're a family with small children is another pain.

Better yet, if you ever built a new home, you know how annoying it is to drive back and forth watching your dirt and waiting for them to start with the foundation, framing, roof, etc.   Later on in the book, we will share how we addressed this pain.

Once you have figured out your customers' pains you can then address them in clear marketing messages that make your customers sit up and take notice.

To give you an example of how this works, let's compare two moving companies.   Below, in Figure 3.1, is a collection of Yellow Page ads from local moving companies.

Figure 3.1

Most of those below feature headlines with the phrases "local and nationwide moves," "family owned and operated" and "free quotes." Pretty standard wording, right? The same wording you'll find in most advertisements for movers.

After working with a client, we created this ad, Figure 3.2, that takes an entirely different tack. It opens with the simple phrase "We won't break your stuff."

Figure 3.2

A recent industry survey stated the number one concern (and therefore the number one "pain") of people hiring a mover is the "safety of their belongings." Knowing this, the new company directly addresses that concern. Now when choosing between the two, the consumer selects the company they connect with because they offer a real solution to their problems or challenges.

In addition to the great headline, the ad goes on to talk about the company's well-trained staff, its insurance coverage, and its "double your money back" guarantee, which is "If we break it, we pay you twice its value!"

After taking the time to hear this company's simple but direct pitch, it's obvious that this is the only company for consumers to trust with their valuable belongings (and also the only company to do business with!). Want to test this idea? Open up your local Yellow Pages and see the ads for movers. We predict you'll be underwhelmed.

How does all of this relate to you? Take a moment and review your current marketing material. Is the message clear? Does it address the pains that your clients have? Does it explain why your company is the "only" choice to solve their problems? Probably not. But isn't recognizing the problem the first step to fixing the problem?

If your marketing isn't working, it probably isn't all your fault. What you're doing (not even realizing you're doing it) is copying your marketing style from a long history of big business branding.

Your ad agency or graphic designer is creating ads that look nice, and maybe contain a cute phrase and photo, but don't do the best job at accomplishing the task at hand – getting people to notice you, listen to your message, and *spend money with your company*.

Show us a marketing piece that has won creative awards and we'll show you a piece that probably didn't produce at the cash register.

Many companies invest a lot of money in marketing programs that never work. These programs don't work because they're NOT grounded in reality. They look good, but they don't consider the customer. While this might work for a Fortune 500 company with a humongous advertising budget designed to build name recognition, it's not going to work for you.

Your marketing must be built on a foundation that first considers your customers' perspectives, opinions, challenges, and pains when buying a product or service from a company like yours.

It then takes those pains and translates them into strong messages and headlines that enable people to directly relate to your company – and how ONLY you will be able to solve their specific challenges.

An example of a business owner who tried the Reality Marketing™ approach is Barrett Ersek, President of HappyLawn.com. HappyLawn.com is a provider of lawn fertilization, aerating and insect protection to homeowners. He had a new tree and shrub protection service to offer his lawn-care customers, but he needed an effective approach to explain the value of this service to them.

His first attempt was to offer the new service based on a discounted price – trying to show how cheap it was to protect a

Reality Byte

Competing on Price or Service

Many entrepreneurs compete on price, even though this strategy hinders the performance of new ventures, which are better off competing on service, quality, or some other dimension."

Scott Shane

Author of *Illusions of Entrepreneurship: The Costly Myths that Entrepreneurs, Investors and Policy Makers Live By*
New Haven: Yale University Press.
http://wsomfaculty.cwru.edu/shane/

customer's trees and shrubs. He used postcards and telemarketing to get the word out and received nominal response to his "$39 per month" offer.

When he came to us, we did a small phone survey to existing clients and quickly realized it wasn't the cost of the *service* they cared about. Instead, they were terrified of the replacement cost should all of their trees and bushes die from disease or weather.

The strategic message was obvious. It's cheaper to sign up for HappyLawn's protection service than replace the trees!

Using this approach, a tactical plan was devised to attack HappyLawn's customers. A trifold brochure was produced featuring a sad homeowner complaining of his loss and explaining how he spent $14,896 to replace all of his trees (ouch!). It further described how easy it was to protect the trees and bushes using HappyLawn. We teamed this brochure with promotional mini tree saplings that the HappyLawn staff hand delivered to existing clients in targeted neighborhoods. The first day produced 42 subscriptions!

OK, now we've talked about how companies execute a Reality Marketing™ program for a business to consumer (B2C) company. Let's talk about business to business (B2B) applications.

One of our clients was a national provider of Sarbanes-Oxley consulting services. With the new Sarbanes-Oxley laws, public companies are required to hire an independent firm to review their internal and external accounting procedures to verify accuracy.

When we first started working with this client, her marketing messages focused on the fact that she had 10 offices around the country to service clients. Her main marketing strategy included expensive print ads in financial trade magazines targeting chief financial officers. This was very expensive and relatively ineffective.

After an initial introduction to Reality Marketing™, she realized there was a better way to reach her target clients. We decided to reconstruct her campaign using a Reality Marketing™ approach that identified the pains of the target group (CFO's or the audit committees).

Those pains included a time constraint associated with getting audit controls in place. Without these controls, their firms could face large fines and penalties from the government. Using those pains, we developed a campaign that promoted a free report on "Six ways to create an effective Sarbanes-Oxley compliance program in 30 days".

The content in the report was delivered through a series of web casts. (Note: Web casts are an easy way to hold a workshop in a virtual manner. Using an outside vendor, you arrange for attendees to view a presentation, with sound, right from the comfort of their own desktops, while you conduct the presentation right from your office.)

She created a hard-hitting presentation tailored to CFOs and other public company officers via this free web cast, offered once per month and promoted through a series of regular e-mails. She invited prospects to sample this "seminar" and learn more. This did three things.

First, it self selected the prospects with a need for her services.

Then, it built a prospect list of registrants or people interested in hearing her messages.

Finally, the event positioned her as an expert in the field by giving information that people need to make a smart, informed and educated decision.

All in all, a gigantic switch from expensive, non-performing advertising tactics to Reality Marketing™ tactics that slashed costs, drove sales and built a prospect database.

Reality Marketing™ is easy to execute once you change your mindset. Later in this book, we are going to take you through a step-by-step process to create your own Reality Marketing™ system.

Start Today! Tips

1. Take a look at your Website to review whether it addresses your prospects' concerns or "pains."

2. Look at your toughest competitors' Websites and compare them to yours.

3. Create an online survey and ask your clients what "pains" your product or service solves for them.

Chapter 4
MARKETING INSANITY

Insanity is defined as "the expectation of different results from doing the same thing over and over again." So what is "marketing insanity?"

Marketing insanity occurs when a business owner, entrepreneur or marketer keeps looking for a different result from the same ineffective marketing tactics that they insist on repeating over and over again. In our practice, many business owners have come to us with this malady – and no idea how to cure it.

We've heard a million reasons over the years for why business owners keep at these losing tactics. The owner who thinks he has to be in the Yellow Pages because otherwise "people will think I'm out of business" (as if there are thousands of us out there with nothing better to do than track the Yellow Pages!).

Or the owner who keeps running newspaper ads that don't work because it "keeps her name out there" (the purpose of business is to make money…keeping your name "out there" and losing money is the most frustrating thing we've ever heard).

The answer to curing marketing insanity is of course data – lots of data.

When we advise a client on the marketing mix required to generate leads and sales, we always include the most vital ingredient – testing and tracking. Heck, let's find out what's working and what's not.

Sometimes our clients have sophisticated databases where they tag new prospects with a code that indicates how they got to the company. Other times, it's as simple as taking a clipboard and a pen and making tally marks every time a new lead comes in and recording what source generated the lead.

The secret to tracking and testing understands that if you're going to spend money doing multiple marketing activities, finding those that *actually produce a result is* imperative.

Here's our suggestion to you. For the next week or two, monitor how people are introduced to your company. If you have an active business and you are always getting new opportunities to introduce your services or products to clients, then you should have enough data to realize which marketing tactics are working and which aren't. Figure 4.1 shows an example of what this information should look like.

Marketing Event	Calls/Emails	Meetings	Proposals	Actual Sales	Expected Sales	Winner or Loser?
Direct Mail To Prospects	43	17	7	1	3	Loser
Email Marketing	128	51	20	7	6	Winner!
Printed Newsletter	26	10	4	1	4	Loser
Trade Shows	229	92	37	9	9	Winner!
Print Ad Campaign	12	5	2	0	3	Loser
Workshop Series	168	67	27	9	10	Winner!
Telemarketing	600	240	96	19	8	Winner!
Referral Mailing To Clients	10	4	2	1	6	Loser
Totals	1216	486	195	48	49	

Figure 4.1

Too many times, the business owner will say, "I think we get a good response from our Yellow Pages ad." However, when we start to track it, the complete opposite is true.

It seems that business owners cling to the latest information available to them (the last order, the last call), and ignore longer-term data that shows over time what method produced the most leads.

Once these sources have been quantified as to what they produce, it's time to make some hard decisions. Sometimes, even a favorite marketing technique, such as a billboard Is a billboard a "technique"? or a radio ad, makes the owner feel good because of ego or pride. But yet, when we track it, it does not provide the results that it should based on the amount of money being spent on that tactic. Sometimes the most boring and affordable techniques provide the best results.

We once had a client who was executing marketing projects with a very poor return on investment. We decided to try a very "guerilla marketing" oriented Google AdWords pay-per-click campaign (the sponsored links on the right side of a Google search screen). We set the budget at $50 per week.

At $50 per week, qualified prospects were finding our client's Website at the rate of two or three times per day leading to one sale per day. Certainly not earth-shattering results, but for the $50 investment, a fantastic return on marketing investment.

Once we gauged that this was actually bringing in a steady flow of leads for a reasonable cost, we decided to ramp up the program. Now, the client has cut other marketing expenses and put in place a $1,000 per month pay-per-click program. Now, he has all of the opportunities he needs to reach their sales goals.

Not only is our client generating more and more leads, but his cost per lead has been driven down. No, a Google Ad Words program isn't as sexy as a billboard with the name of the company emblazed on the side of the highway, but the program is generating profit and that is a direct cure for most "marketing insanity."

Start Today! Tips

1. For just one week, start to track every call or e-mail you get from new prospects so you can determine where most of your leads come from.

2. Create a system to review new marketing tactics 30 days after they begin to see if they show signs of success.

3. Look to immediately eliminate any and all marketing tactics that you are using that don't have a quantifiable and positive return on investment.

▌Chapter 5
GET OUT OF YOUR COMFORT ZONE

Now that we've got you thinking a bit differently about your company, it's time to visit one of the biggest business killers. It's the comfort zone, as shown in Figure 5.1.

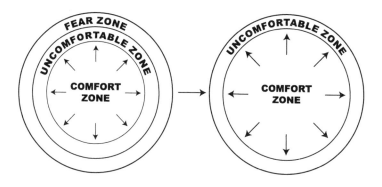

Figure 5.1

Like a well-worn recliner in the basement rec room, your comfort zone can be a nice place to live.   Soothing, calming, and reassuring. The comfort zone makes you feel…well…safe.

But in the business world, staying in the comfort zone is dangerous.

Why? Because it means you aren't trying anything new.   It means that you're sticking with strategies that aren't working and you're continuing to run campaigns that aren't producing customers.

To be blunt, staying in the comfort zone won't get you anywhere near your goals and objectives. To succeed in this new world of marketing, you must be willing to yank yourself out of your comfort zone and try something new.

Let us give you two examples involving two very different clients.

The first was a home builder. Each week he would take out an $800 ad in the local newspaper, but wasn't really sure how it was performing. When he became our client we began to track how many calls came in from the ad. It turns out he averaged just two calls a week, with only a few of them actually turning into clients. That's an acquisition cost of $400 per lead. Unacceptable!

It wasn't long before we recommended that he stop running the ads because they weren't working. His reply: "I can't do that." When we asked him why, he said "because every builder *has* to be in the Sunday newspaper." He continued running the ads and we ended the relationship a short time later.

This builder wasn't willing to break out of his comfort zone. Against all common sense, he *had* to be in the newspaper even though he knew quantifiably he was wasting a lot of money and bringing in almost no customers. He wasn't even building a prospect database.

Remember, you don't *have* to do anything. This isn't high school where you do what everyone else is doing because it's cool. This is the business world and you're in business to make money. Assuming that's your goal, the only thing you *should* do is put your money into tactics that focus on bringing in customers who spend money!

Our second example involves the owner of a large pre-owned luxury car dealership. Every month, he spent more than

$6,000 to run small classified ads in newspapers for the cars in inventory. During our first meeting we asked, "How is the response to those ads?" When he replied "not very good," we asked him why he kept running them. His answer: "Because my competitors are and I don't know what else to do."

We immediately recommended he stop the ads and try something different. If nothing else, he would at least save $6,000 a month! He agreed and we got to work. After analyzing the last 100 deals they did, it was obvious that practically all of his business came from referrals and repeat customers.

We went on to create some campaigns that focused on those areas. We created monthly "Cool Car Rallies" so existing clients could test drive different models. The price of admission? One prospect! Now you had prospects mingling with happy clients and live testimonials. The cost of the rallies were a few snacks and the printing of some road maps highlighting the test drive route.

We also started an e-mail campaign with existing customers to keep the company front of mind as their leases were expiring. By telling the clients stories about how the company helps people, the e-mails cross sold additional services like repair and detailing services. By moving out of his comfort zone, this owner was able to use more effective marketing strategies for a fraction of the cost.

There's a saying about people who suffer from addictions. That they can't begin recovery until they admit they have a problem. That's what the comfort zone is like.

Until you are ready to admit what you're currently doing isn't working, dump your ineffective marketing strategies and try something different, you'll be doomed to a lot of wasted time and money.

Get out of your comfort zone…NOW!

Start Today! Tips

1. Research two methods of marketing not previously utilized by your company.

2. Call three potential partners with whom you could exchange leads and contacts.

3. Call a customer that didn't choose to use your company and ask them the honest reasons why.

Chapter 6
IT'S ABOUT THEM (NOT YOU)

Like everyone else, business owners like to talk about themselves. That's fine if you're at your 25th high school reunion but can be a disaster if such chattiness appears in your marketing materials.

Why? Don't take this personally, but…people just don't care.

We know that sounds harsh but it's the truth. Very few consumers are sentimental. Most only care about what you can do for them and how you help them solve their problems.

It doesn't matter whether you've been in business for 75 years or that you're a family-owned and operated company or that you just took delivery of a whiz-bang new piece of equipment. What they care about is how you're going to make their lives easier.

Look at the millions of people who stopped going to family-owned hardware stores when Home Depot came to town. Or all of the quaint Main Street businesses that closed shop after Wal-Mart moved in and offered everything under one roof at a discount. People naturally gravitate to businesses that ease their pains and make life easy.

One of the biggest mistakes companies make in their marketing materials and advertisements is the overuse of "we." As in, "we are the leading widget maker in the city" or "we specialize in taking on big jobs."

Frankly, my dear, who cares? You need to tell customers what you'll do to ease *their* pains. It's like the concept of "oversharing" sometimes less truly is more.

The good news is, it's easy to start marketing the right way.

To help our clients change the focus of their marketing material, we employ what we call the red/blue test. Simply take marketing information – a letter, Website, e-mail, advertisement or whatever – and print it out. Then, using a red pen, circle every reference to you or your company—usually indicated by the words "we" or "our," or your company name. Then, using a blue pen, circle every reference to how you're going to make your customer's life easier – usually indicated by the words "you" or "your," or our clients.

Figure 6.1 provides a visual example. The sales letters designate references to "you" as squares and the "clients" as circles. Notice how many more squares there are than circles in the original sales letter.

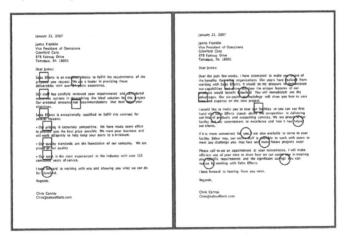

Original Sales Letter   Revised Sales Letter

Figure 6,1.

The best marketing pieces have a lot more blue/circles than red/squares. More blue means you're talking to consumers, letting them know that you understand their problems and are offering them solutions. Too much red means you're speaking about you and not letting the consumer know how you're going to fix their problems. Remember, your <u>customers only care about what you do for them.</u>

They are uninterested in a new piece of equipment, but only care about what it does to help them; as in, "Will my order be delivered on time?" It makes no difference whether you've been in business for 10 years or 10 months, only that you continue to meet their needs. They don't care that you're the No.1 widget maker in the city, they want to know how that No. 1 ranking benefits them.

One great way to change your focus from "we" to "you" is to get to know your customers better. Many business owners can talk at great length about their company, their production schedule, or the features of a new product, but can't honestly say what those mean to their customers.

To find out what your clients do care about, go out on some sales calls. Do an informal survey. Work the front desk periodically.

When you start making these inquiries, you'll find out what your customers' day is like, what roadblocks they come up against, and how you can make life easier for them. By knowing this information, you can better write marketing messages that will speak directly to customers.

Remember, if you want it to be all about you, go to a class reunion.

If you want to make money and have a successful business, write marketing materials that speak to customers' needs and they'll feel like writing you checks!

Start Today! Tips

1. Perform the red/blue test on all of your marketing materials.

2. Call three clients and ask them for suggestions for products or services that they would like to receive from your company.

3. Review your communication processes to see if you can make it easier for your clients to connect with you.

4. Call your own company to see how easy it is to do business with your team.

Chapter 7
I WISH I SOLD MOZZARELLA CHEESE!

When we talk to groups of business owners about marketing, we often tell them that we wished we sold mozzarella cheese. Why, you might ask?

For one thing, we would know precisely who our primary market was – pizza parlors. Our marketing plan would be easy – we'd hit every pizza parlor within an ever-expanding radius, service the heck out of them, and then we'd be done.

Our point? You need to identify your target market.

Once you've done that, stick to aiming your ads and marketing messages *only at that market*. Unfortunately, it's not always as easy as it is for the mozzarella cheese salespeople.

At our workshops, we go around the room and ask eachbusiness owner to identify his or her target market. A typical response, like this one from an owner of an ink cartridge refilling company, is usually something like, "Everyone who owns a printer."

Does he mean everyone in America who owns a printer? "Oh no. Just those in the Philadelphia area." OK, now we've quickly narrowed his focus to one geographic region.

Next question: What if the purchasing manager at a huge Philadelphia company with thousands of printers asked if you could service their entire business? "We couldn't handle that large of an account." OK, so now we're focused on small- to medium-size companies in the Philly area.

Not exactly… "Most of our business is with individuals or very small companies with five printers or less." Now we're getting somewhere.

We won't go into all the other questions we asked this man, but suffice to say that the longer we probed the owner about his business and customers, the more defined his target market became. The eventual description was "office managers at small and medium-sized businesses within a 60-minute drive from the store."

Now, try doing the same for your business. When going through this exercise, do not assume you know your market. Remember, the ink cartridge guy initially said his market was "everyone who owns a printer." If you stop at a blanket statement like that, then you haven't delved far enough.

Invest considerable time in this exercise. Mull it over, discuss it with your employees or even do a simple survey among customers and employees. You want as narrow of a market as possible.

Once you figure out *precisely* who you want to target, you can then spend your time and marketing money aiming your messages at them and only them. This allows you to focus your limited resources and budget on only those people who offer you the opportunity to grow your business.

One last point about the ink cartridge guy. When we asked him if he would take an order from Chicago he said "Yes." Which is fine, even if he is located in Philadelphia. That's gravy. What you should *not* do, however, is start spending your time and money aiming your marketing at Chicago. This man's market is Philadelphia. If and when he has conquered Philly, *then* he can turn his attention to Chicago.

According to Geoffrey Moore, the author of *Crossing the Chasm*, business owners are usually faced with multiple target markets, such as a wholesale and a retail division. Each one of those target markets requires a separate conversation or marketing approach. The wholesale customer gets a different story about the company than the retail customer. Moore's concept is illustrated in Figure 7.1.

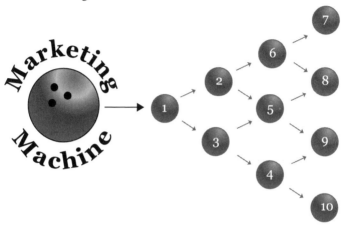

Figure 7.1

So which target market should you go after first? Think of your customers as bowling pins: when you're getting ready to throw the ball, you try to attack the lead pin (No. 1), focusing your energy and resources on knocking that pin down or conquering that target market. The momentum you get from success in the first target market then carries over to the second target market (pin No. 2) and the third target market (pin No. 3).

The relationship between the pins and their sequence is important. As with bowling, the energy from the lead pin contributes to knocking down other pins. In the selection of the first target market, the others have to be defined in a way that allows them to relate. For example, if your first target market is the VP of human resources at large pharmaceutical companies, your next target market could be the CFO at large pharmaceutical companies, or the VP of human resources at biotech companies. There is a relationship, or bridge, that will allow you to leverage your success in the initial market with the second or third market.

We've yet to meet the client who has exclaimed, "We have an unlimited marketing budget! Let's go after everybody at the same time with equal fervor!" Because all clients have limited marketing budgets, we need to make sure we knock down the most obvious and powerful pin (that provides the easiest sales and biggest profit) and then use the energy from that to knock down the next one.

The following are four case studies whose target markets are identified and discussed here and in Chapter 8. Names have been changed to protect the innocent!

Home Trust Mortgage Company

Phoenix-based Home Trust Mortgage did a little of everything – car loans, primary home mortgages, home equity loans, and so on. The owner knew her business was unfocused so she decided to concentrate on what it did best—helping homeowners in Phoenix consolidate their credit card debt though home equity loans.

Target market: Phoenix homeowners with debt issues.

Precision Architects

Precision Architects outside of Miami pretty much took anyone who walked through the door and lacked a clear marketing strategy and focus. So the firm's partners decided to aim their services at existing homeowners who required more room.

Target market: Single-family homeowners who need additions and renovations in the Miami metro area.

Friedman Sales Consulting

When he launched his business, Sam Friedman of Friedman Sales Consulting liked to say that if you were

Reality Byte

Turn Your Competitors into Your Sales Force

After giving a speech to a business group recently, I was reminded by one of the participants of an unexpected benefit of finding a safe little market niche. Many established businesses that you might normally think of as your competitors can become your sales force.

Find a niche that is a part of the market that established businesses don't really want to serve. The customers may be too small for their operation, or serving them may be just too inefficient for their size. I have seen this recently in new law practices, landscapers, healthcare, web design, food distributors, etc., etc. Look for needs to serve not just in customers, but also in the businesses already established in the market.

What seems like crumbs to them can become your feast. Actively market to them. You will make them look good, as they will have an easy referral outlet for business that does not fit their model. That keeps them looking like a good guy to their referral sources.

Dr. Jeffrey Cornwall
Author of *Bringing Your Business to Life*
Director of the Center for Entrepreneurship
Belmont University
http://forum.belmont.edu/cornwall/

in sales, you were his customer.   He marketed himself to individual salespeople as well as Fortune 500 companies.

He claimed he could help people learn how to sell, dress, speak, and develop leads.   But Sam cast his net too wide, and was unable to capture any market share at all. So, to get his business back on track, he decided to specialize in one area – small business owners and their sales teams in New York City.

Target market: Owners of small businesses (companies with less than 20 employees) in New York City who need more sales.

Little Italy Restaurant

Since opening two years ago, Little Italy Restaurant has tried to cater to everyone – old, young, couples on dates, big groups, families, etc.   Business was OK but not spectacular, primarily because it had never established a solid identity.   It was just one of dozens of decent Italian restaurants in the area.   To carve out a niche and help it stand out, the owner decided that Little Italy should be known as offering relaxed dining for families with young children.

Target market: Area families (within a 10-mile radius) with school-aged children and younger.

You, too, will need to spend time thinking about your business's identity and target market.   To help you stay focused, try to identify your market in five words or less. Once you've done this, you'll know exactly who and where to target your message and marketing will become much easier.

The worksheet in Figure 7.2 will help you with your own target market selection process.   For an electronic version, visit www.realitymarketingrevolution.com

	Target Market 1	Target Market 2	Target Market 3
Geographic Criter			
Individuals characteristics (titles if B2B)			
Size firms or size of household			
Industries			
Unique Issues			
Profit potential			
Other			

Figure 7.2

While a light bulb can light an entire room, a laser can cut steel. The power that comes from focusing directly at your target market is awesome. It helps you utilize all of your available resources to conquer a specific target market. Once you have claimed victory over that one, move on to the next. It's the only way companies with limited maketing budgets can have a competitive edge.

Reality Byte

Bob's Rules

Pay attention to your competitors, but pay more attention to what you're doing. When you look at your competitors, remember that everything looks perfect at a distance. Even the planet Earth, if you get far enough into space, looks like a peaceful place.

Bob Parsons' 16 Rules for Success in Business & Life in General
Founder and CEO of Godaddy.com
www.godaddy.com

Start Today! Tips

1. Evaluate the kinds of clients who contribute most to your revenue and especially your profit.

2. List all of your present target markets as well as goal target markets in the near future.

3. Identify the titles of the buyers you want to sell to (e.g., Vice Presidents of Sales).

4. Complete the target market definition worksheet on shown in Figure 7.2 or found on the www.realitymarketingrevolution.com Website.

▍Chapter 8

IDENTIFY YOUR CUSTOMERS' PAINS

Once you have identified your target market, the next step is to figure out what problems, challenges, or issues keep your prospects up at night. We refer to these as "pains." Chapter 3 identified a person's pain as being related to your specific business, product, or service.

The easiest and quickest way to figure out what pains your customers have is to talk to them – work the front desk; go on sales calls; answer the phones; talk to your friends, relatives, and neighbors; write up a brief survey and ask your customers to take it. In short, do a little research. Don't obsess with making any of this scientific. The point is simply to take the pulse of your customers.

Your prospects' real pains can be less than obvious and may not always be the first issue that comes to mind. With the homebuilder client in Chapter 3, the prospects' pains weren't how to afford the home, or getting the needed features. Their pain was driving back and forth from their old home to the site of their new construction to make sure it was proceeding on schedule.

Following are the four companies whose target markets were identified in the last chapter. Now let's figure out their customer "pains."

Home Trust Mortgage Company

Based on the results of a simple phone survey, the owner found that the majority of her customers carried large balances on their credit cards and couldn't handle the monthly payments. That's why they were seeking the debt consolidation services of Home Trust.

Customer pain: I can't make my monthly debt payments and it is causing stress and angst.

Precision Architects

Since the target market for Precision Architects is going to be single-family home owners who need additions to their houses, the pain for this market was relatively easy to figure out.

Customer pain: "Our kids' toys are all over the place, we need more room!"

Friedman Sales Consulting

Figuring out the pains in Sam Friedman's market – small companies in New York City that want to double their sales – was a little less obvious. After all, small business owners have a lot of pains, right? After talking to a number of clients, however, he realized that their primary concern was being able to pay their bills and meet payroll.

Customer pain: "I need more sales so I can pay my bills and make payroll."

Little Italy Restaurant

Now that Little Italy had decided to focus on family dining, the owner did a quick, informal survey of his friends and relatives with children. Almost unanimously they all agreed that eating out with children is a problem because of long waits and, as a result, fussy kids that prevent them from enjoying a pleasant meal.

Customer pain: "Get us in and out quickly or entertain our kids so they enjoy the wait."

Like the four business owners, you'll need to spend time thinking about the real issues or pains facing your prospects and customers. A good rule of thumb is to identify at least three pains for each of your target markets. Once you identify the pains, talking about how you can help solve them or creating solutions makes your marketing more effective and helps your business stand out from among the rest.

The worksheet sample provided in Figure 8.1 will help identify customer pains. For an electronic version of this worksheet visit www.realitymarketingrevolution.com

Target Market 1	
Pain Statement 1	
Pain Statement 2	
Pain Statement 3	
Target Market 2	
Pain Statement 1	
Pain Statement 2	
Pain Statement 3	

Figure 8.1

Now that we have pain statements for our case studies, the next step is to write working headlines that address the target audience's pain. These are designed to grab your prospects' attention so they will use your company's product or service.

Are headlines just for print ads? Obviously not. When we use the word "headlines" we're talking about a strong opening statement that encapsulates the essence of what you can do for your client. This builds upon the five-word-or-less description of the target market discussed in the last chapter. Remember when creating your company's headlines, you want to be able to sum up a prospect's pain in just a few words.

These headlines should be found on all marketing materials. Headlines are to be used on the home page of your Website, a subject line of an e-mail campaign, print ads, and even custom lettering on the sides of vans.

For the four cases, we created the following working headlines which addressed customer pains:

> **Home Trust Mortgage Company:** "Isn't there a company that can help us understand how to consolidate our loans?"

> **Precision Architects:** "I just can't visualize what this addition is going to look like. Not to mention how much it's going to cost!"

> **Friedman Sales Consulting:** "I need this to work <u>now</u>. How will I know if this consultant is really helping me?"

> **Little Italy Restaurant:** "I can't bear another crazy dinner where my kids are acting up! There must be a child-friendly restaurant nearby!"

Figure 8.2 will help you convert your pain statements into working headlines for target customers. For an electronic version of this worksheet visit www.realitymarketingrevolution.com

Target Market 1	
Pain Statement 1	
Headline	
Pain Statement 2	
Headline	
Pain Statement 3	
Headline	

Target Market 2	
Pain Statement 1	
Headline	
Pain Statement 2	
Headline	
Pain Statement 3	
Headline	

Figure 8.2

Start Today! Tips

1. Think of and list all of the questions that prospects ask when contacting your company the first time.

2. Select the three most important pains and write them in this form "Who can help me..." (e.g. "Is there an accountant who can help me minimize my tax implications?). Use the form in Figure 8.1.

3. Poll your clients to verify those pains. Did they have these issues before working with your company? Have you been able to help them solve their pains?

Chapter 9

BE REMARKABLE

"That won't work here." "We tried that once." "We can't do that." We hear these phrases all the time from business owners and other prospects. It's a good thing none of these people ever worked for Walt Disney.

When Walt held his staff meetings he challenged those in attendance to dream of what they *could* do instead of telling him what they *couldn't* do. In fact, he insisted upon it.

For example, one of Walt's ideas was to make his theme parks look brand-new every single day. His team initially scoffed, "That's impossible! We'd have to paint and scrub the park every night!" Well, guess what, that's exactly what they do and it's one of the reasons the Disney theme parks are such a smashing success.

The Dreaming Room was created by Walt Disney and has been discussed extensively by Michael Gerber, author of the *E-Myth* and *E-Myth Mastery*. When you're in the Dreaming Room (which doesn't have to be an actual room by the way) there are no stupid ideas and no excuses. For us, the Dreaming Room is where you let your mind wander and come up with ideas that will make your business remarkable. We use it all the time when working with our clients.

The concept of making your business "remarkable" was initially introduced by Seth Godin in his book, *The Purple Cow*. What he means by that phrase is that you must find those characteristics about your business that will set you apart and make people talk about you. For instance:

> It's a beautiful day outside of your office and your staff is feeling a little stale. You decide to go for a drive in the country. Everybody piles in the car and you drive through the rolling hills and countryside. One person says, "There's a cow!" You all look. Then another person says, "There's another cow!" You all look. After a while, all of the brown cows seem to blur together. Then someone shouts, "There's a purple cow!" What do you do?

> You stop the car. Get out and go to the fence. You call people and tell them where they can find the purple cow. You snap photos on your camera and e-mail them to people, showing them the world's only purple cow. Before you know it, there are 200 people by the fence all amazed at the purple cow.

The story of the Purple Cow has several analogies. First, most businesses are brown cows. They are scenery, blending into everyone's day-to-day lives. No matter how loud or often that cow moos, it's never going to get the attention of the passing drivers.

Your job as business owner, entrepreneur, and marketer is to turn your company into a "purple cow." A business that is so remarkable that people start talking about it.

Here is one example of what we mean by "remarkable."

If you've ever built a new home you know how often you have to drive to the work site to see its progress. This invariably takes a lot of time and is a hassle, but seems like the only way to see how construction is coming along.

But what if the builder installed a $49 webcam at each of the lot sites? That way, the builder's customers could log onto his website anytime and see an updated picture of their house as it was constructed. Not only does it save gas and is eco-friendly, but it eliminates the time and trouble of driving back and forth. Brilliant!

The customers loved the service so much that they shared their log-in information with all of their friends and family members so that they, too, could also watch the house being built. Traffic increased on the builder's Website, customers were thrilled with the additional (and unexpected) service, and positive buzz began to grow.

This builder understood his customer's pain. He came up with a solution and in the course of his actions, made his business remarkable.

Here's another example. We have a client in the tool rental business. He specializes in carrying big tools and equipment for contractors – jack hammers, generators, fork lifts, and back hoes. It's a family-owned business which has done things the same way for years. Contractors would park their vehicles out front, come in, wait in line, tell the guy at the desk what they wanted, fill out a bunch of paperwork, and then pay. They then returned to their vehicle and drove it around the back, got out again, and helped load the equipment onto the vehicle. The whole process took approximately 30 minutes each time.

Very little about this business made it stand out from the other rental companies in town. However, they were open to new ideas (in our figurative Dreaming Room) and were willing to move out of their comfort zone, as discussed in Chapter 5.

To make the company remarkable, we suggested that it reorganize the hassle and wasted time during rental pickups and try a new service called "fly-by pick-up." Using this service, a contractor drives right up to the back of the building where she is met by a company representative. The contractor, who now has an account with the company, already phoned in the order so it's waiting when she arrives. Company employees have the equipment cleaned, oiled, and prepped for delivery. They quickly load the equipment into her truck, she signs a receipt and is on her way. What used to take a minimum of 30 minutes now takes only 3. The contractor never has to leave the vehicle, doesn't have to stand in line and saves 27 minutes of valuable work time. Remarkable! Once the word spread about this excellent service, new contractor customers starting switching from their other rental companies.

Our last example involves a bowling alley. To compete with many entertainment options available today, this particular alley needed to be remarkable in some way. So the owner installed software that allows patrons to log on to the company's Website, reserve a lane and shoes, enter in all of the bowlers' names and charge the whole thing to their debit or credit card. When the game was over, the system automatically e-mailed the scores and an analysis of the game to each bowler, along with a coupon for another visit. As an added bonus, because the alley was now collecting people's e-mail addresses, it was building a rich customer database for marketing purposes to promote birthday packages, their new billiards room, or a "guys night out" program. For literally pennies per e-mail, they can identify the right people and talk to them about the solution to their entertainment issues. Now that is Reality Marketing!™

We could go on with dozens of examples of companies that have found ways to make themselves remarkable. One thing all of these businesses have in common is that they are ordinary. In fact, on the surface, most are pretty routine – a homebuilder, a tool rental company, a bowling alley.

But what they have in common is a desire to identify their

customer's pain and then create a way to stand out from the crowd. In short, they've found a way to be remarkable.

Can you think of how to position your company as remarkable? It's important to do so; otherwise, you might end up like everyone else, an ordinary business in a field of brown cows.

Reality Byte

Shop Owners Need to Hit the Streets Too

Sometimes retail shop owners have the "open and wait" mentality. I put my stuff out, run some ads and wait, right?

Well, that does work for some, but if you're finding that it doesn't work well for you or that all this talk about a downturn in the economy is keeping people away, then maybe you need to hit the bricks a bit.

Just today a gift basket shop owner wrote to me and asked what she could do to get more traffic. I advised her to network and go look for strategic partners. (This is really good advice no matter the industry) It probably sounds a little foreign to some retailers, but a little out of the store hustle goes a long way.

So, our gift basket shop owner would approach businesses and show them how to use her product to generate more referrals and create customer loyalty. A flower shop could approach a remodeling contractor and suggest a customer wow program that involved sending a bouquet of flowers thirty days after a project is finished. (Now of course there's nothing to stop you from reaching out to the florist and suggesting a reciprocation of some manner as well.)

There are literally hundreds of ways to approach this strategy. The key is to frame the partnership around what your potential partner wants. It's never about you and your business, show them how to use your products and services to get more of what they want.

Keep at this kind of relationship building and your business will be recession proof.

John Jantsch
Duct Tape Marketing
For more information and tips, go to:
www.ducttapemarketing.com/blog

Start Today! Tips

1. Make a list of all of the things you feel are remarkable about your company.   If a competitor can say the same thing, cross it off and think of something else.

2. Identify companies you feel are remarkable and see if you can transfer some of their tactics to your company.

3. Come up with 8-10 remarkable aspects of your business. It may seem difficult, so use your creativity. Thinking of something new and unusual that distinguishes your business from the rest is the most important part of your new approach to marketing.   So keep at it!

▌Chapter 10
CURE YOUR CUSTOMERS' PAINS

If you read just two chapters or do only two sets of exercises in this book, it should be this one and the next. Chapters 10 and 11 contain the secret of successful marketing and can help you go from marginal to "remarkable."

However, this will require a great deal of probing. While it's relatively simple to decide who to target and find out what their pains are, creatively solving their problems and differentiating your business is hard work. And unfortunately, many businesses think their people, their reputation, their experience, and their product are "good enough" to make them successful. But there is always someone who is saying the same thing as you are, even if it's untrue. To your prospects, it sounds exactly the same.

This is where Reality Marketing ™ comes in. We will help you create a remarkable company that does it better, faster, and cheaper than your competition because you have x, y, and z which they of course do not possess. This is the most important concept in this book and the secret to great marketing. Every business provides some product or service, but it's <u>how</u> you deliver that product or service that makes your business special, and ultimately drives the success of your marketing.

So if you are looking for the proverbial silver bullet, this is it. Work hardest on making your business remarkable in every way possible and the rest will fall into place. Take shortcuts, or the easy way out and you may find yourself throwing away tens of thousands of dollars in traditional advertising to grow your company only marginally, if at all. So make sure you have something remarkable to say to make the best use of your advertising dollars.

How you cure your customers' pains are what we call *solutions,* steps each business takes to make customers' pains go away. Innovative solutions are the first step in becoming remarkable. The four sample companies discussed in earlier chapters illustrate how to create solutions that go directly to their client's pains. Are these solutions remarkable?

Home Trust Mortgage Company

Now that Home Trust's owner knew her customers and their pains, she needed to develop a unique solution to ease their difficulties. So she created a simple, one-page Web application that they could fill out online. Within approximately a half-hour of completing it, customers would be told how much they could borrow to consolidate their loans.

Unique solution: Fast, hassle-free access to a consolidated loan approval.

Is this solution remarkable?
❑ YES
❑ NO (Many other companies offer this general service)
Let's try again.

Unique solution: Instapproval™ via Website for fast, hassle-free access to a consolidated loan approval decision in just 29 minutes.

Is this solution remarkable?
❑ YES (A specific and less stressful solution that distinguishes it from the pack
❑ NO

Precision Architects

To address their customer's pain of needing more space, the firm's partners first had to realize that the solution required more than producing blueprints for the homeowners. Every architectural firm did that. What they needed was something to help them stand out from the crowd.

So the partners purchased software that allowed the firm to produce a computer-generated, 3D view of what the addition would look like, along with an approximate cost...all within 48 hours. While most firms took weeks to get back to the client with a cost estimate and two-dimensional drawings, Precision was able to offer their clients almost immediate feedback.

Unique solution: In 48 hours, an architect presents accurate real-life designs or mock-ups of their addition along with an approximate investment estimate.

Is this solution remarkable?

❑ YES (most definitely; it greatly speeds up the process and adds an extra "dimension")
❑ NO

Note: If the investment estimate is too high for the prospect, then they have actually "pre-qualified" themselves *out* of the process, saving them time and money trying to close a deal that will likely never happen.

Friedman Sales Consulting

Since Sam Friedman's target audience wants to double sales, he decided to organize his presentation into a clear, concise package for customers.

Unique solution: 12-point sales training program that guarantees results in 90 days.

Is this solution remarkable?
❑ YES
❑ NO (somewhat limited in scope)

Let's try again.

Unique solution: 12-point sales training program that guarantees initial results in 30 days and an ongoing training ensures long term results.

Is this solution remarkable?
❑ YES (much better – results are sooner, with a long-term guarantee)
❑ NO

Little Italy Restaurant

After he determined his customer's primary pain, the owner of Little Italy needed to cut down the wait time for a table. So he invested in an online reservation system. Now parents with small children can reserve a table from home, show up at the appointed time, and be seated within five minutes, guaranteed.

Unique solution: Online reservation system that greatly reduces wait time.

Is this solution remarkable?
❑ YES
❑ NO
MAYBE (But what about customers who are less computer savvy? Only a certain percentage could take advantage of it, thus limiting its effectiveness.)

Unique solution: An online reservation system and the ability to pre-order your meal over the phone. Now there isn't any waiting at the table either, and the meal arrives soon after you get your drinks. A kids' play area, with games, books, and a movie also help out those who didn't make online accommodations.

Is this solution remarkable?
❑ YES (Much better)
❑ NO

These examples illustrate how important it is to push an idea to its very limits. Even the best good idea can be challenged to be better, to be remarkable. The opposite of remarkable is ordinary, which makes your company just like the rest of the brown cows discussed in the last chapter.

The final step then is to write *marketing messages* or headlines that address the target audience's pain and offer a solution. We introduced this basic concept of headlines in Chapter 8 and discussed how these messages are used on all marketing material, advertising, websites, and so forth.

Marketing messages and headlines encapsulate the essence of what you can do for your clients, not only attracting their attention but focusing on their emotions and hinting at your remarkable solution.

For example, a cleaner was trying to attract new customers through print ads. Using the Reality Marketing™ methodology, we uncovered that nobody likes to physically go to the dry cleaner. Almost everyone hates the whole experience – rushing to get there within the dry cleaner's limited hours; waiting in line with a heavy armload or basket of smelly, dirty clothes; lugging an equally cumbersome package of clean clothes back home; and doing most of this in nasty weather. As it turns out, not one of these pains had anything to do with coupons or even saving money.

However, the company offered free VIP pick-up service at no additional charge at the customers home or office every Tuesday or Friday morning. The customer's didn't even need to be present, as long as the laundry was clearly identified and left in a designated spot. To make it even more convenient, all services were billed to a credit or debit card.

Along with being unique, the service solved many client problems, so we encapsulated it into a strong headline, "Never set foot in a dry cleaner again," as illustrated in Figure 10.1.

Figure 10.1

This headline and solution are not only brief and powerful, but address the client's pain at physically having to drag heavy loads of clothing to the dry cleaner. It also piques their curiosity as to *why* they never have to go there again. The supporting copy in the ad explains why this is a better way to do business.

Chapter 8 also discussed using just one phrase to sum up the unique ways to help clients in creating your company's headlines.

For the four cases, we came up with the following solution statements.

Home Trust Mortgage Company: "They approved us instantly, and I slept peacefully, knowing my bills will be paid."

Precision Architects: "In just one visit, they showed us exactly what our new family room would look like and about how much it was going to cost us."

Sam Friedman Sales Consulting: "In just 30 days, we increased our sales pipeline by 212% and doubled our close rate!"

Little Italy Restaurant: "Our kids were happy the entire time and it was the most peaceful dinner out we've experienced in years!"

Although it will take a lot of poking, prodding, and research to get to, the solution can be a simple one. You don't need to hire a consultant for tens of thousands of dollars. Do the extra leg work and talk to your customers to find out how you can make their lives easier. Then you can start to come up with clear-cut solutions.

Start Today! Tips

1. Make a chart listing all of your customers' pains on one side and your company's matching solutions on the other.

2. See if your solutions are unique to your company versus those of competitors.

3. Verify that clients actually care about the solutions you provide.

Chapter 11

NO-RISK VS. LOW-RISK OFFERS:
THERE IS A DIFFERENCE

At the beginning of this book we said that two-step marketing – you advertise, customers buy – is dead. There's just too much market noise out there that prevent your message from getting through.

In today's competitive market, you have to give the public a *reason* to buy your product or service. Then – if they are interested or when they have time – consumers will select what *they* want, when *they* want it. We live in a self-service, instant gratification world and potential customers are tuned into this.

While this may frighten business owners who pine for the old days, it's actually a great opportunity to create strategies to get around that noise or, better yet, cut through the clutter and reach your target market.

One of the most powerful strategies is the " no-risk offer". This is quite different from a *low-risk offer*, which is a free quote or initial consultation. To get that free consultation, prospects have to make time in their busy schedules. They might get lost on the way to your office or you might be late to their house or place of business. Plus, when they meet someone new, people are generally uneasy. They may fear you might put the "hard sell" on them or that they will be obligated to buy after the consultation.

While none of these things are earth-shattering, you can see that there is clearly a risk for the prospect to initially get involved with your company.

In contrast, a *no-risk offer* is simply free information that you will gladly give to someone in exchange for his or her contact information, such as an e-mail address.   No meetings, no obligations, no talking.   If the person wants to get the information at 2 a.m. while they're in their pajamas, they can easily do that.

What you're doing is letting them come to you.   Your lure is the free offer.   If they want it, they can take the very slight risk of giving you their contact information.   If they aren't willing to give you their contact information, they aren't close to being ready to purchase anything from you.

The purpose of collecting contact information or e-mail addresses is to build a large prospect database full of people who have stepped forward, raised their hand and said "I'm interested in the kind of product or service you offer."

For example, if you own a moving company you might offer a "Free Packing Prep Guide," knowing that anybody requesting one is considering an upcoming move and is a potential customer.   Once you have secured the contact information from the person who downloaded or was mailed the free guide, you then begin to market your business to him or her. Before you know it, you will have a prospect database of hundreds or thousands of people who are interested in moving.   All you, as the business owner, have to do now is explain in a series of regular communications all of the wonderful things that your moving company does versus the competition.

For example, the no-risk offer on the Website of an executive recruiting company is, "Nine things you must know BEFORE hiring a search firm."   Think about it, if I came to their site, I probably am planning on hiring such a firm.   Now I can learn even more about my search. So everyone who downloaded that file is a prospect. We just moved them from anonymity to prospect in 1.2 seconds. Now *that's* marketing.

Instead of having to advertise to the whole world with little or no return, this company can now spend time (and much less money) marketing itself to its database of prospects.

- Any business can provide a no-risk offer. Here are a few more examples.
- An accountant offers a one-pager about "Six ways to minimize taxes."
- A mortgage company offers "What the other guys won't tell you about getting a mortgage."
- A family restaurant provides a booklet on "73 table games for fidgety children."
- A dry cleaner provides tips on "10 ways to remove tough stains."

The point isn't to give away so much information that the prospect doesn't need your services. Rather it's a foot in the door and a way to begin building a robust database of potential clients that have an interest in your business. And, through continuing education, you distinguish your company as an authority in its subject matter.

So how do you get started? Think about a topic that troubles your prospect when considering a purchase of your product or service. Then write a tip sheet, free guide, white paper, collection of stories, or anything else that might appeal to that potential customer. The information should always be educational or informative.

Post it on your Website and have your sales people offer it for free when networking or prospecting. Most importantly, only give out this valuable information in exchange for someone's contact information. Put the contact information into a database and start to mail, e-mail, or call to continue the conversation with the prospect.

However, there are some caveats to no-risk offers. If you call prospects, it should always be with their prior consent – you don't want to come across as being a telemarketer or a nuisance. If you launch an e-mail campaign, be judicious in the e-mails that you send to your database. You don't want to bombard them with ads or give them an impression that you are a spammer. They will automatically delete your e-mails without even opening them or worse yet, unsubscribe and end the conversation.

By keeping your phone calls, e-mails and other correspondence brief and informative, you become a trusted advisor and someone who will help them ease their pains. As customers ourselves, we find it refreshing when we receive information that is useful to us rather than something that hits us over the head to make a sale.

And of course you should still provide low-risk offers such as free quotes and consultations to potential clients. These should continue to hold an important place in your marketing plan. But they should be undertaken *after* customers have received and accepted the no-risk offer, when they feel comfortable to take communication to the next level. Figure 11.1 shows the progression of a sale through these various steps.

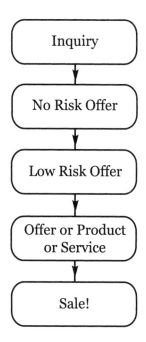

Figure 11.1

So first, provide potential customers with a no-risk offer. Once you have their contact information and they have received the informative materials from you, then you can go ahead with low-risk offer. You'll be another step closer to doing business with them and making the sale.

Start Today! Tips

1. Review the list of pain statements and pick one that you hear the most in your business. Create a list of five tips or hints that help your clients deal with this pain. Write them down.

2. Now go back and write a couple of sentences or a paragraph or two on each of the five tips or hints. Format the document nicely with your logo, Website, e-mail address and contact information.

3. Review the document and give it a catchy name, as suggested by the examples in this chapter. Test market it with established prospects and clients to get their reaction.

4. If feedback is positive, post the report to your Website and offer it to prospects and clients in exchange for their contact information.

5. Track how many new e-mail addresses you get.

6. If the first document doesn't attract much traffic, revise it and keep test-marketing it until you find one that performs best.

▌Chapter 12
THE MARKETING MACHINE™

The machine is one of the great marvels of the industrial age, especially those where raw materials are fed in one end and a final product produced out the other. It's a bit like magic. Wouldn't it be great if there was such a machine to help you with your marketing? Just feed it your raw materials – like messages and potential customers – and out pop leads and sales.

But guess what? A Marketing Machine™ really does exist! Rather than being a physical piece of equipment that you can purchase, it's a metaphor for an integrated marketing program that takes a potential new business inquiry (the first time they hear about your company) or suspect from Point A and ends up with a sale at Point Z. Between those two points are marketing tactics or programs you can use and the various communications you have with prospects.

But in order to understand how potential customers move through the Marketing Machine™ they need to be identified and include the following:

People (businesses) in the target market.
They may or may not be aware of your business.

Suspects. These are people in your target market who <u>are</u> aware of you. They may have even visited your Website, read a brochure, noticed your ad, or provided you with contact information.

Prospects. These people have expressed an interest in doing business with you and your company, but have not progressed beyond the interest stage.

Leads. These people are about to make a purchase decision. You are typically actively engaged with them by providing quotes, answering questions, or negotiating terms.

Closed sales. These people have given you money in exchange for your services. They are now your customers!

It's important to understand the degrees of potential and actual customers because the Marketing Machine™ excels at moving people in your target market through each of these stages.

Customers are drawn to your business in three primary ways – <u>advertising, public relations</u> and <u>referrals</u>. Many companies intrinsically understand this but then don't do anything after a person becomes a suspect or someone who has heard about their company. An all-too-familiar example of a failed Marketing Machine™ is the company that spends tens of thousands of dollars to exhibit at a trade show and then comes home with 200 business cards and leaves them in a shoe box on the corner of their desk. It's sort of like loading the raw materials into your machine and then failing to turn it on.

For example, a replacement window company advertised extensively on TV, radio, and print. The ads generated tons of phone calls. Unfortunately, the company only wanted to deal with leads— people who were interested in immediately purchasing windows.

If callers just asked for a quote or for more information (these kinds of requests made up 75 percent of their phone calls by the way) the company didn't want to spend time dealing with them.

In fact, the company didn't even capture the contact information for a prospect database. In essence, this company was throwing away 75 percent of its leads or all of its suspects and prospects! Its Marketing Machine™ wasn't broken, it didn't even exist.

The first part of the Marketing Machine ™ should capture contact information on *everyone* who calls your company. This information can then become your company's prospect database, which along with prospects and leads, also includes suspects. Your prospect database is one of your biggest assets. Protect, grow, and nurture it. It will provide you customers for years to come if you handle it properly.

In Figure 12.1, if Point A is "collect their name and e-mail address," then Point B would be "call them back to follow up." Point C would be "send them a brochure." Point D would be "send them an e-mail." Point E would be "another follow-up call." Point F would be "invite them to a free seminar" and so on. Figure 12.1 also illustrates how multiple contacts with your target markets will help move suspects to prospects, prospects to leads, and leads to new to clients.

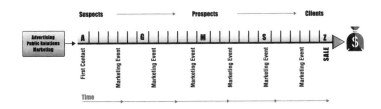

Figure 12.1

What most marketers and almost all business owners don't realize is that the potential customer is in control of the process. Big ad agencies tell you that the more you advertise the more likely people will buy. However, the truth is potential customers will only buy when their pain becomes acute.

So how do you deal with this? Again, big ad agencies often say you need more ads, but is that really necessary? *The only time a traditional radio, print or TV ad attracts a potential customer is when their pain becomes acute.* The planets literally have to align for that to work.

But with a Marketing Machine™ you have more control over the process. Say you sign up for a trade show to meet potential customers. When the prospects arrive at your booth, it is their first contact with your company and the beginning of the Marketing Machine™. This would be Point A in Figure 12.1 when they're first introduced to your company.

The challenge is that the suspect or prospect already has a vendor who is offering similar services. And right now, they are relatively happy with the vendor, who ships most of the orders on time. So there is no pressing reason for them to change.

The relationship between the companies has been going on for a while, making the pain associated with switching seem significant. While the prospect is interested in what you have to say, their current relationship is acceptable enough that they don't want to switch. On top of that, they have five other business issues they need to deal with anyway.

Does this sound familiar? At this point, most people give up and never talk to the prospect again, thinking they are not worth it since they already have a vendor. But a company with a Marketing Machine™ looks at it differently. They collect contact information and start to market to them in a regular rhythmic manner. Not selling, but educating, sharing information, and working to help the prospect be better at their job.

The first month, they send an e-mail. The second month, they send a postcard. The third, they invite them to a Webinar, a Web-based educational event similar to that discussed in Chapter 14, and so forth, slowly and subtly building the case as to why your company should take over as the new vendor. During the entire time, your prospect is dealing with their current vendor.

But given the law of averages and the fact that you are dealing with many suspects or prospects in this manner, opportunity eventually knocks. And your prospect's current vendor drops the ball on a really large order and 50,000 pieces that were supposed to be ready by the first of the month instead arrive on the 10th. And your prospect is livid. Guess what? Their pain is now acute!

To paraphrase the movie *Ghostbusters*, "Who are they gonna call?" You, obviously, because since you met them at a trade show, you've been telling them all along how and why your company is remarkable. And they kept listening until the time was right because what you had to say helped them in their business. So when their current vendor dropped the ball on that 50,000 piece order their pain became acute and they came to you. There was no need for an extensive search for a new vendor, since they already knew you, your position, your advantages, and what made you remarkable. So, they called you instead!

Because we never know when the pain is going to be acute, it's imperative to keep communication flowing so you're involved in the prospect's decision-making process. Therefore, you want to keep communicating with these prospects until either:

- Their "pain" becomes so acute that they buy your product or service

- They buy from someone else and ask to be removed from your Marketing Machine™

One of the keys to the Marketing Machine™ is regular and rhythmic communication with your prospects. Oftentimes, when companies start to work on their marketing, they get a couple of big orders and then think they don't need it any more.

However, this is hardly true. For example, if you own an ice cream parlor, chances are you're very busy between the months of June and August. You're so occupied you don't do any marketing. After all, why do marketing when you're busy, right? But in September, a cold spell hits and your business drops off. *Now* you decide to do some marketing. That's the wrong approach.

You should be doing marketing year-round, *especially* in the summer when the people who eat ice cream are ready to buy your product. You never know when a prospects' pain will become acute enough to need your services. Even marketing in the off-season will build a case why your suspects or prospects should do business with your company when the weather turns.

For instance, say an architect met with a potential client about an addition to her house. When the prospect found out the cost would be $60,000 she backed off. Her pain wasn't acute enough yet to make the investment required for the addition she envisions. As the family continued to live in the house, however, it became more and more cramped. All the while, the architect kept marketing to the client on a regular basis. Then one day the client's aunt passed away and left her a nice inheritance. Suddenly the client had the money for an addition and was ready to return to the architect. If the architect hadn't been communicating regularly with this client, he would have risked losing her to a competitor.

You also have to create the right size Marketing Machine™. If you have lofty sales goals, you probably need a bigger, more comprehensive machine. If you have minimal growth goals, you might only need a machine with only a few tactics.   The key here is to construct a Marketing Machine™ directly related to your company's goals and objectives.   Chapter 13 will discuss this concept.

A word of caution about the Marketing Machine™—it can be frustrating for companies with very long sales cycles.   That's because the machine doesn't produce sales overnight.   However, if you own such a company, feel confident that the longer the sales cycle, the more time and better chance you have to build your case using the Marketing Machine™.   In such instances Marketing Machines ™ may even significantly shorten the sales cycle.

For instance, a business that builds, owns, and manages offices for small companies such as medical practices or insurance companies can have a highly successful Marketing Machine™. This company finds land and puts up a structure "on spec" and targets commercial real estate brokers and small business owners within 20 miles of that particular building. Because this company never knows when a potential client's pain becomes acute and because the sales cycle can be long, it frequently offers a "free office-leasing guide" and "free tips on how to negotiate a lease," to its large prospect database.   Throughout the year, the company communicates regularly with its database, sending postcards and e-mails, calling them, offering free tips and inviting them to open houses.   The result is a cost-effective marketing program (Marketing Machine™) that generates a consistent flow of leads.

Finally, the replacement window installation company mentioned earlier in this chapter got wise to the Marketing Machine™. Instead of letting 75 percent of its prospects disappear, it now collects the information and adds it to a database.   Throughout the year, the company communicates regularly with this list and has turned suspects into prospects, prospects into leads, and leads into customers.

And replacement windows, while having a long lead time, can be lucrative. They would generate an extra $1.2 million a year in revenue if they added just one more order a day from the database with an average order of $4,000 per customer.

Could you use an extra million?

Start Today! Tips

1. Compute the amount of leads (and sales) you will need to achieve your sales targets.

2. Make a list of the tactics that you think should be in your Marketing Machine™.

3. Allocate the number of new leads from each of these programs and then based on the actual sales calculate the number of new customers you can expect from these programs. If the number is low, consider using some additional marketing tactics.

▌Chapter 13

AM I READY FOR A MARKETING MACHINE?

Nearly every business could benefit from a Marketing Machine™ approach. However, setting it up and in motion requires a considerable amount of work. Some of the tasks have already been discussed in earlier chapters.

Before you begin, take this short quiz to help determine your level of readiness.

1. I am ready to "think out of the box" and try some different marketing approaches.
   ❑ True
   ❑ False

2. I clearly understand who I want to be selling to, where they are, and what makes them tick.
   ❑ True
   ❑ False

3. I have a few strong pain statements that clearly capture my target market's challenges, pains, or issues related to my product or service.
   ❑ True
   ❑ False

4. I have converted those pains into strong headlines for use in my marketing materials.
   ❑ True
   ❑ False

5. I have at least five strong competitive advantages that make my company/product/service remarkable.
   ❑ True
   ❑ False

6. I have created a compelling no-risk offer to collect new prospect contact information.
   ❑ True
   ❑ False

7. I have a prospect database to collect all contact information regardless of how they come into our company.
   ❑ True
   ❑ False

8. Our company is prepared to track the performance of all our new marketing programs and be active in their measurement and management.
   ❑ True
   ❑ False

If you answered "True" to six or more questions then you are ready to build your Marketing Machine™. If you only answered "True" to 3-5 questions, then you are on your way, but may need to reread earlier chapters before starting. Less than that, you might want to re-think your commitment to this entire exercise.

For anything to work, you should be open to suggestions for change and willing to move out of your comfort zone. Say your company is currently at Point A and you want to grow it to Point B, as shown in Figure 13.1. The area of increase – C - will likely make you feel uncomfortable. Which is perfectly normal, since you have never been in this uncharted territory before. You'll need to work though this feeling to take your company to the next level.

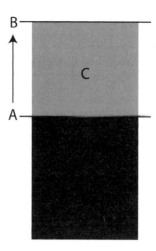

Figure 13.1

The next step towards building a Marketing Machine™ is to clearly define your goals and objectives. The following series of questions will help you determine whether you have done this, so it's important to answer them honestly and accurately.

1. What is your sales volume for the current year? $_____

2. What is your target sales volume for the next year? $_____

3. What is your average sale? $_____

4. Your gross profit margin is _____ percent

5. How many leads do you typically get in a year? _____

6. What is the ratio of total leads to sales (leads that have closed, _____ percent?

7. How many new visitors come to your Website each month _____?

8. What was your total investment in marketing during the past year? Make sure you include signage, Websites, brochures, and other marketing-related services. $_____

9. Make a list of all your current marketing activities

_____
_____
_____
_____
_____
_____

Now that you have this information on paper, you are ready to start making the calculations for your Marketing Machine™. The following example, filled out by Home Trust Mortgage Company, helps illustrate the process.

1. What is your sales volume for the current year? <u>$2,340,000</u>

2. What is your target sales volume for the next year? <u>$3,000,000</u>

3. What is your average sale? <u>$80,000 contract results in an $8,000 commission</u>

4. What is your gross profit margin? <u>About 25 percent</u>

5. How many leads do you typically get in a year? <u>10 a month or about 120 for the year.</u>

6. What is the ratio of leads to sales that have been closed? <u>About 20 percent</u>

7. How many new visitors come to your Website each month? <u>On average, 100 a month.</u>

8. What was your total investment in marketing during the past year? Make sure you include signage, Websites,

brochures and other marketing related services. <u>Last year, we spent a total of $123,500.</u>

9. Make a list of all your current marketing activities <u>Website, signage, postcards, community outreach, cold calling, local newspaper ads, occasional e-mails, holiday cards, refrigerator magnets, and Chamber sponsorship of one breakfast.</u>

Subtracting Question 2 from Question 1, we know we need incremental revenue of about $700,000 to reach next year's goal. If we consider the revenue from commission, and typically make about $8,000 per deal, we are going to need 87 more deals next year.   Since we close 20 percent of all the leads, we are going to need 435 leads.

So our Marketing Machine™ needs to increase the number of leads from 120 per year (10 a month) to about 435 a year or about 36 a month.   That is a pretty big leap.   It's doable, but it's going to require a larger Marketing Machine™. Figure 13.2 illustrates the Home Trust Mortgage Company Marketing Machine™

Marketing Programs	Number of Expected Leads
Marketing Plan	No leads, but required to understand, pains, solutions and what makes company remarkable
Website Redesign and Development	10 a month; 120 a year
Pay Per Click Advertising	5 a month; 60 a year
Monthly E-mail	6 a month; 72 a year
Lead Referral	2 a month; 24 a year
Electronic Brochure	2 a month; 24 a year

Public Relations	4 a month; 48 a year
Educational Workshop	8 a month; 96 a year
TOTAL	**37 a month; 444 for the year**

Figure 13.2

Based on the above example, it's perfectly reasonable to expect more leads as a result of implementing the package of programs outlined in the Marketing Machine™. However, there are other ways to improve performance and get to goals. What if the owner was able to improve his close ratio from 20 to 30 percent? That would make a significant impact. Looking closely at your marketing plan and making sure it's solid and clearly defined can not only give you new ways of achieving goals but can also lead to strong, measurable results.

 Start Today! Tips

1. Take the first quiz in this chapter to make sure you are ready. If you answer "True" to two or fewer questions, take a hard look at your business, your goals, and your passion for the business.

2. Take the second quiz to help you define your goals and objectives. If you don't know all the answers, keep doing research until you do.

3. Try to come up with some elements of your Marketing Machine™.

Chapter 14

HOW TO BUILD AND EXECUTE YOUR OWN MARKETING MACHINE™

If you followed the methods outlined in earlier chapters, you have already done much of the heavy lifting. You have the key messages, you worked to make your business remarkable, you understand the pains of your customers and how to satisfy those pains, and you know what clearly makes you different from your competition. We have asked hard questions about your business, prospects, clients, industry, and experiences with the intent of contributing towards a solid foundation for your new marketing efforts.

But from here on, you'll need another element —marketing experience. Although you may have experience marketing your business, it probably hasn't been as successful as you'd liked; otherwise, you wouldn't be reading this book. But here's where we can help.

The tactics included in a Marketing Machine™ are straightforward and have been around for decades. These are the same tactics everyone uses. The art comes in the <u>combination</u> of tactics. The Marketing Machine™ does this effectively, efficiently, and in a performance-based fashion.

As you undoubtedly know, people process information differently. Some like to read, others look at pictures, still others prefer e-mail, while there are those who only act on referrals. Recognizing the different ways your prospects process information is important when building your Marketing Machine™.

Every Marketing Machine™ is different, but to ensure that you are getting to all your potential clients, you'll need a mix of different, complementary tactics held together with a sound strategy. Once you've developed your strategy and messages, you can examine which tactics (or cogs) of the Marketing Machine™ might work for you. Follows are descriptions of the various elements, with examples from our clients.

Web Site Marketing – Holistic Learning Center

The cornerstone of any Marketing Machine,™ your Website must utilize pain statements and solution headlines to drive and engage visitors. You should also provide them with different "no risk" ways to get involved with your company. It's critical, however, to collect their e-mail addresses before providing them any no-risk offers or free reports.

Your Website must always have the most current information on your company. Change it weekly to keep it fresh. Test different messages on the home page and track the performance of your site weekly. Make sure unique visitors, page views, and average time on your site are regularly increasing. Keep fine-tuning it until you see performance improving.

Our client, a holistic learning center, needed attendees for a workshop and wanted to use their Website as a central location for all their educational programming. Their new Website, which included the elements discussed, attracted over 300 attendees. This was accomplished by integrating traditional advertising like print, direct mail, flyers, and brochures into the Website and having all people interested in their workshops go to the Website to register for upcoming events.

E-mail Marketing Campaigns –
Home Renovations and Remodeling Company

E-mail marketing programs are among the best and most effective methods of marketing and the perfect first step in creating a Marketing Machine™. E-mails can be sent for as little as a penny, when you factor in the minimal time and effort involved in preparing the e-mail and sending it to the appropriate lists of recipients for 2 cents each. That means you can send 1,000 e-mails each month for around $10. That's a huge cost savings compared to an average of $500 for the same number of standard-sized postcards.

Also, with the press of a button, you can talk to as many clients or prospects as you want. That is why we emphasize getting the client's e-mail address in exchange for a "no risk" offer or other information. The result will be more customers, more sales, and increased profits.

The sooner you start collecting e-mail addresses, the better. That is why we emphasize getting the client's e-mail address as part of their receiving a "no risk" offer or other information.

Our builder client started with just 88 addresses. After their first e-mail blast, they received a call from a prospect they'd talked to 12 months earlier. The prospect was interested in starting a project the client had quoted during that initial meeting. The final result included a contract worth over $145,000.

Of course, not everyone sees this type of result so quickly, but without an e-mail campaign, your marketing is incomplete and you are missing out on many opportunities to continue talking with suspects and prospects.

Pay-per-click Ad Words Campaigns –
Provider of Vinyl Records

Now that you have a great Website, you have to get people to visit it! This value-based program is proven to improve traffic to your Website by matching people searching for you with your sponsored links. By focusing the paid ad word program on only those key words that directly relate to your business and <u>only</u> paying for actual click-throughs, traffic is delivered in a budget-oriented manner. After the initial strategy is created and keywords identified, this marketing program could be implemented the next day. Typically, people start to see leads in hours, rather than days or weeks.

The more specific your key words, the more effective your ad words campaigns. This client had very specific key words: vinyl records, blues vinyl, jazz vinyl, and so forth. These key words delivered hundreds of click-throughs to their online store. The resulting conversions translated into an increase of about 20 more sales per week, representing a significant improvement with only a modest investment.

Natural Search Engine Optimization Campaigns –
Pet Breeder

The Web is growing at an exponential rate. Every day, individuals use major search engines to launch over 725 million queries for products, services, and information solutions. But how can they find your Website within this vast universe of content? Over 40 percent of all the sites surveyed generated 50 percent or more of their traffic from search engines and directories.

Search engines are the most popular vehicles to connect users to Websites - they provide the very first step in the online communications link. These engines increase targeted traffic from natural search listings on selected key word phrases and convert click-throughs into requests for appointments, additional information, pricing, quotes, or even orders.

Search engine optimization marketing is a great way to significantly increase the number of people visiting your Website. This program requires a six-month commitment to really see the desired returns.

This client wanted to be ranked number one on Yahoo!, MSN, Google, and Ask.com for the keywords "poodle puppies", a challenge at best. As with Google Ad Words, the more general the terms, the more difficult it is because more people are competing for the same words. In certain circumstances, natural search projects are best left to the professionals.

In this case, we were able to rework the copy on their site, add certain tags, and implement other Website changes to deliver page one rankings on both Yahoo! and MSN search engines. These rankings are only temporary and if this is important to your business, plan on updating this on a monthly basis to maintain them.

Banner Advertising Campaigns – Surgical Instruments Wholesaler

Another way to drive people to your Website is to link with other qualified and relevant Websites. This is done through banner ads. For example, a manufacturer of dog accessories can advertise on a site that offers organic dog food. The target market will be similar but the products and services are noncompetitive.

Banner advertising is purchased based on projected impressions. Impressions are the number of people who will see the advertisement. They are also referred to as "eyeballs." This client purchased a three-month contract that was to deliver 3,000 impressions. Based on their data, we expected to get a click-through rate of about 5 percent. On impressions of 3,000, that should be 150 click-throughs to our Website. After monitoring performance for a few weeks, however, we realized the banner advertising program was falling short on expected performance and even though rates were re-negotiated and lowered to reflect the reduced click-throughs, it was eventually cancelled. Remember, all of the tactics in a Reality Marketing™ plan must be quantifiable and must generate a high Return on Marketing Investment (ROMI). Those that fail to accomplish this should be cancelled or at the very least, evaluated and adjusted to improve performance.

Brochures/Electronic or Printed –
Manufacturer of Plush Toys for Promotional Products

It's also critical to create a brochure to help convince prospects to become customers or clients. And while printing that brochure is sometimes viewed as "old school," a digital approach delivers the same visually stimulating marketing material in an on-demand platform and electronic PDF format.

These low-cost materials are used as "sales slicks" describing individual products and solutions for specific target markets, or even to deliver high-level company information. These materials can be used as downloads from a Website, as part of the sales process, or as an e-mail attachment to communicate details during the sales process.

Our client had a variety of product categories. While they didn't want to produce a full-blown printed catalog, they did need sales slicks for certain types of plush toys. They created electronic PDF slicks for each of their standard products for specific occasions such as trade shows, holiday promotions, client gifts, and employee promotions. These pieces highlighted the remarkable aspects of this company and helped the salespeople quickly communicate with prospects. The on-demand nature of electronic PDFs also provides an environmentally friendly approach to distributing marketing material.

Print Advertising Campaigns –
Provider of Upscale Business Meeting Space

Targeted advertising, as executed by newspapers, magazines, and trade periodicals, is an excellent way to promote small businesses. However, these options are expensive. Advertisers pay for each and every person reading that publication. And therein lies the problem: often these readers don't need and aren't ready to purchase what you are selling.

Although there are times when traditional print advertising is a viable option, they are few and far between when executing a Reality Marketing™ approach. So if you are planning this type of campaign, make sure a "no risk offer" is prominently displayed in your ad and that the ad drives visitors to your Website or a specific page therein. This way, you can measure the effectiveness of your advertising.

Our client provided meeting spaces for businesses operating in the northeast corridor of the US. Their meeting space located in Philadelphia was perfect for executives traveling on Amtrak between Boston and Washington D.C. Advertising in Amtrak's *Arrive Magazine* was very specific and targeted and referred readers to the company's Website with an effective no-risk offer.

Client/Prospect Newsletters – Provider of Concierge Medical Practices

Look at your clientele and target market to determine the potential effectiveness of printed newsletters. In this case, a large percentage of the client's customers were elderly, with limited usage of electronic materials and e-mail, so it made sense to create a printed client or prospect newsletter.

However, make sure the information it contains is educational, with articles and helpful tips that help the readers live a better life, do their jobs better, or highlight the personal stories and accomplishments of people of interest to the readers. Never beat them over the head with the expected coupon campaign to take 10 percent off their next order.

Direct Mail Campaigns – Lawn Fertilizer Company

Mailing post cards or letters to potential customers is an excellent marketing tactic. As mentioned earlier, it could become cost prohibitive if the list is extremely large, but if your average sale supports this level of investment, consider direct mail.

Sending a single piece is rarely effective, so plan on doing a series of at least three cards or letters. The design of your card should include your Reality Marketing™ messaging, "no risk offer" and similar Website landing pages as mentioned in the print advertising section. This will help you track the success of the program and allow you to make changes and measure improvements.

In addition to an effective and eye-catching design, the cards should include the offer and the message. The final and perhaps most important key element is that the list consists of your exact target market.

As compared to their previous direct mail campaign, this client's series of cards used the principles of Reality Marketing™ and outperformed the old approach by 10-to-1. The result was a very profitable spring season. An added bonus was the addition of over 1,000 new e-mail addresses to their prospect database. This will make marketing next season easier and significantly cheaper.

Lead Referral Campaigns –
Financial Accounting and Finance Project Outsourcing

Often your greatest sources of leads are current customers. If you provide great products or services, clients and customers only need a little nudge to refer you to others. By making it easy for customers to pass your name along, referrals will start driving sales. This is also related to Viral Marketing on page 106 and can be the start of the "word of mouth" that represents the ideal marketing situation.

This client had a good relationship with customers, so it helped make their referral program a success. They integrated the referral request directly with their sales process by giving printed cards to customers that offered an American Express gift card for every referral that turned into a project. Now, after a project starts, sales people ask their clients for referrals as part of their standard operating procedure.

Public Relations Campaigns – Retail Soft Pretzel Company

It's one thing to say your company is great through your marketing. It's another if people read about it in the local paper or better yet, hear about it on radio or TV. Public relations (PR) provide great exposure for your company.

But to get a story in the media, you need something interesting to say?, and not just something that fascinates you, but catches the eye of the reporter or editor. Our client won "Best of Delaware and Philadelphia" for their delicious soft pretzels. To take advantage of that award, we created an event, the Great Philadelphia Soft Pretzel Give Away!—free pretzels for anyone who came into the client's store on a certain day. To grab the media's attention, we sent a box of fresh soft pretzels to all the TV stations. We also invited them to broadcast live from one of the retail outlets. The result was four separate segments on the morning news.

The media attention drove Website traffic up a whopping 205 percent, resulted in a collection of 231 new e-mail addresses in just one day, and an increase of e-mail requests for franchise information from 2 to 11 during the week of the event. When done well, nothing works better than a strong public relations program to make your marketing efforts "pop."

Event Sponsorship – Professional Services Firm Specializing in the HR Industry

Sponsoring an event can be a great investment in hitting a specific target market. For as little as the price of a lunch, you can speak in front of a captive audience of your most highly targeted and profitable prospects. You position your company as the experts and the obvious choice to do business with.

However, securing the right event sponsorship requires some research. Find out the events and groups that your prospects frequent, then offer to sponsor a lunch, networking meeting, or breakfast session. The rest can be like shooting fish in a barrel.

Our client wanted to talk to VPs of HR from local companies. We contacted the local Society for HR Managers (SHRM) and asked if they had any opportunities for our client to sponsor upcoming events. They suggested the client speak at an upcoming lunch. After preparing a short presentation, our client made a number of new contacts that resulted in several engagements. All that was invested was the cost of soda and sandwiches.

Trade Show Campaigns –Company Specializing in the Development of Ambulatory Surgical Centers

If you sign up for a trade show, forget the expectation that by your mere presence, attendees will beat a path to your company's booth. Rather you need to maximize your investment with a strong plan.

Trade shows are expensive, sometimes costing over $10,000 for a large national event. This includes booth space, materials, and any extras like electricity and Internet connectivity used at the show plus the cost of travel, food, and lodging for a minimum of two employees. So if you are going to spend that money, make sure to get a significant return on the investment. You'll need a comprehensive and well thought out plan to drive attendees to your booth. A show theme, pre-show mailing, post-show mailing, and a promotional give-away that tie directly to your theme should work together to convey a strong message that you have the cure for your customers' "pain." So you have a lot of work and preparation ahead of you before you even set foot inside the trade show.

Our client was to attend a show in Washington D.C., but lacked a specific marketing plan. So we quickly coached them on ways to optimize their investment by setting goals for each day in terms of both collecting e-mail addresses and identifying qualified doctors who might be interested in opening up a center. We also created a fun and engaging contest to attract attendees to their event space, all the while collecting their contact information so the client could continue to market to them via e-mail after the trade show was over. The results: collection of over 100 qualified prospect e-mail addresses, five opportunities for new potential centers, and an overall positive experience for our client.

Educational Workshop Campaigns – Square 2 Marketing (That's us!)

Educational workshops are a great way to not only validate you as an expert in your field but place you in the best possible light in front of customers and prospective customers. A good example of an educational workshop is our own program. We started it years ago in the back room of a local restaurant, with only 30 people attending the event. But every three months like clockwork we regularly scheduled, promoted, and delivered our workshop. Today, an average of 70-80 people attend our events, resulting in 3-5 qualified leads for our sales team to pursue.

You can easily institute a similar program. Remember to start small and keep it consistent. Rather than pushing how great your company is, focus on helping the attendees resolve their problems and come up with innovative ways to help them that will improve their business (using your product or service, of course).

Webinar Development – Data Center Services and IT Consulting

Similar in nature to the educational workshop program, this project provides a platform to communicate with qualified prospects without incurring the costs associated with traditional seminar or workshop events.

Delivered via the Internet, Webcasts allow executives to share stories and details of their offerings with up to 200 people. Along with eliminating the hassle and expense of travel, Webinars also provide prospects an opportunity to engage with you, ask questions, and satisfy their desire to learn more about your product without leaving the comfort of their desktop.

Reality Byte

10 Ways to Triple your Profits!

1. Learn how to use the pillars of the great religions to have prospects more than buy from you, use them so that they will have faith in you and close the door on all of your competitors.

2. Perfect the art of never, ever looking like you are selling anything.

3. Deploy the timeless and irresistible power of creating an ironclad guarantee, a guarantee in you.

4. Take objections and boomerang them back to the prospect as opportunities in disguise. This takes you out of the business of sales and into the role of solution provider.

5. Position yourself as a professional, a trusted adviser, and once you attain this vaunted position-and we'll show you how to claim it-the prospects pursue you.

6. Be a mesmerizing story teller, wonderful stories that engage and capture prospects.

7. Rid yourself of the crutches of Power Points, catalogues and product samples. While you are playing with these gadgets, your prospects are losing patience and respect by the minute.

8. Don't ask the prospects what they need. That's a loser's gambit. Instead, tell them what they need. They don't want to be interviewed. They want to be informed and guided.

9. Introduce the element of surprise. Tell prospects what they don't expect and you throw them off balance. And that's precisely how you want them.

10. Control the agenda. Once the balance of power shifts to the prospect, it is game over.

Mark Stevens
For more information and tips, go to
http://msco.com/blog/

This client offered a Webinar on eliminating hot spots within a data center. Through their marketing, which included a significant amount of e-mail blasts, they were able to get over 70 registrants. As a result, they obtained three very lucrative opportunities for potential customers.

Web 2.0 Marketing – Square 2 Marketing (Us Again...)

The Internet is a constantly changing environment. Web 2.0 is a popular term that attempts to describe some of its recent changes, enhancements, and growth. As opposed to a viral program that includes a lot of legwork to post items across a variety of different media, Web 2.0 involves the use of technology as a core component of your Website.

Some of these technologies include blogs, RSS feeds, Podcasts, video, Universal Search, and strategies to automatically present content to sites like Reddit, Digg, Del.icio.us, Flickr, mySpace, and YouTube.

Our firm posts Podcasts of our Reality Marketing™ radio shows to iTunes and our own Website. We create videos with tips on how to improve marketing and not only also include them on our Website, but also on YouTube. We have a blog with daily updates on some of our most interesting projects. Our Website offers an RSS feed with hundreds of subscribers.

Although again it takes extra time and effort, you might consider including similar tactics for your company. Using these sophisticated media can result in a tenfold increase in traffic to your Website.

Telemarketing Campaign – Product/Service Providers

Often you need a bridge between traditional sales efforts and marketing programs. A structured telemarketing campaign coupled with creative marketing tactics can significantly improve performance of traditional telemarketing efforts. What we call a *10-10-10 program* is extremely effective in helping sales people gain appointments with targeted prospects and building your e-mail database.

After key prospects are identified, <u>10</u> introductory calls are made to announce the delivery of a package, <u>10</u> packages are overnighted, and <u>10</u> follow-up phone calls are made to discuss the package, make initial contacts, and secure the appointment.

What's key is creating an interesting package that directly relates to the "pains" of the target prospects. For example:

- A package of cookies in an empty milk carton to illustrate the matching ability of a temporary staffing firm.
- A full-color retractable banner for a large-format color printer.
- A bottle of jelly beans in a prescription bottle for meeting planners tired of "lame meeting syndrome."

Be creative but true to the rhythm of your Marketing Machine™. So if each of your three sales people made 10 phone calls, sent 10 boxes, and followed up with 10 key prospects for just 40 weeks a year, that would result in your company creatively reaching out to 1200 of your most important prospects. With those kinds of numbers, chances of closing at least a few opportunities are pretty high.

Viral Marketing Campaigns –Good for Everyone!

Viral marketing (word-of-mouth marketing) is both low-cost and extremely efficient, thanks to validation from third parties. Just think about it— instead of spending an insane amount of money on newspaper ads, TV commercials or banner ads, you spend nothing—and let your fans do all the work for you.

With viral marketing, word of your product, service, or company suddenly gets a life of its own—and starts to spread like a virus. Everyone wants to see it and when they do, they all want to share it. It is immensely powerful, usually having 500 times greater impact than regular advertisements.

The key to a strong viral campaign is original content and a remarkable story. You really do need to have something that people <u>will</u> talk about. Once you do, it's about putting that content in front of "sneezers;" that is, people who spread word about your product, service or company just like a virus. These can be industry leaders, the media, or anyone in the field who others listen to and respect. They can also be large groups of regular consumers, who happen to like your product or service.

Individually, each of the programs discussed in this chapter will have only minimal success. But together, structured in an orchestrated manner they provide the combined power of a Marketing Machine™.

However, every one that you implement must be monitored, just as you would with each investment in a stock portfolio. That way you'll know which ones succeed and which ones fail.

Now that you have the details on these tactics, think of ways to bundle a few programs together to build your own Marketing Machine™.

Start Today! Tips

1. Compute the amount of leads (and sales) you will need to achieve your sales targets.

2. Make a list of the marketing tactics that should be in your Marketing Machine™.

3. Allocate the number of new leads from each of these programs and then based on the ratio of actual sales, calculate the number of new customers you can expect from these programs. If the numbers are low, you might need to do more marketing.

4. Select the marketing tactics you need for your Marketing Machine™.

▌Chapter 15

MEASURING PERFORMANCE OF
A MARKETING MACHINE™

In Chapter 4 we talked about marketing insanity. This occurs when a business owner, entrepreneur, or marketer keeps looking for a different result using the same ineffective tactics over and over again. The solution to marketing insanity is lots of data; that is, find out what's working and what's not. We call this Return on Marketing Investment, or ROMI.

When we talk to people about ROMI we tell them about our Golden Rule: The money spent on a marketing program must be <u>significantly</u> less than the money earned from that program. For example, many business owners look at a $1,000 marketing campaign that brought in $1,000 in revenue and say they "broke even." If they bring in $2,000 they say they "made money." Not true! They're forgetting to factor in are all of their expenses – the cost of their time, the cost of the goods sold, and so forth.

Before you figure out your Return on Marketing Investment (ROMI) you need to know three numbers:

Your gross profit margin (if you sell a product for $1, what it actually costs you to produce; say, 20-30 cents)

- Your administrative expenses (everything else besides the cost of goods sold – heat, rent, phone, salaries, consultant fees, etc.)
- Your marketing budget

The result can be found on the ROMI chart on Figure 15.1 below.

Marketing Event	Cost Per Year	Expected New Clients	Expected Revenue	Net Revenue From Program
Direct Mail To Prospects	$9,000	3	$15,000	$6,000
Email Marketing	$1,500	6	$30,000	$28,500
Printed Newsletter	$10,000	4	$20,000	$10,000
Trade Shows	$5,000	9	$45,000	$40,000
Print Ad Campaign	$10,000	3	$15,000	$5,000
Workshop Series	$2,000	10	$50,000	$48,000
Telemarketing	$100	8	$40,000	$39,900
Referral Mailing To Clients	$9,000	6	$30,000	$21,000
Totals	$46,600	49	$245,000	$198,400

Incremental Sales	$	245,000
Cost of Goods Sold (60%)	$	147,000
Gross Profit Margin	$	98,000
Administrative Expense (14%)	$	(34,300)
Subtotal	$	63,700
Marketing Budget	$	46,600
Contribution to Net Profit	$	17,100
ROMI - Return on Marketing Investment		37%

Figure 15.1

Although the 37 percent ROMI looks promising, consider Figure 15.2.

Marketing Event	Cost Per Year	Expected New Clients	Expected Revenue	Net Revenue From Program
Direct Mail To Prospects	$9,000	3	$15,000	$6,000
Email Marketing	$1,500	6	$30,000	$28,500
Printed Newsletter	$10,000	4	$20,000	$10,000
Trade Shows	$5,000	9	$45,000	$40,000
Print Ad Campaign	$10,000	3	$15,000	$5,000
Workshop Series	$2,000	10	$50,000	$48,000
Telemarketing	$100	8	$40,000	$39,900
Referral Mailing To Clients	$9,000	6	$30,000	$21,000
Totals	$46,600	49	$245,000	$198,400

Incremental Sales	$	245,000
Cost of Goods Sold (65%)	$	159,250
Gross Profit Margin	$	85,750
Administrative Expense (18%)	$	(44,100)
Subtotal	$	41,650
Marketing Budget	$	46,600
LOSS	$	(4,950)
ROMI - Return on Marketing Investment		-11%

Figure 15.2

This chart shows in jarring detail what happens when you're just a little off on your metrics. Only a few small changes in the numbers can have a big affect on the bottom line. So it's important to know your <u>exact</u> expenses.

Tracking the return on your overall investment in marketing is critical. But you also need to track performance of individual marketing programs and think about your mix of marketing programs.

Consider how you might handle a stock portfolio. When you buy a stock, you purchase it with certain expectations. Some people even put stop orders to control risk. If the stock rises or declines to a certain level, it's automatically sold. This strategy is effective with equities. It's even more reasonable for marketing programs.

For example, if I am going to invest $1,000 in a 30 day pay-per-click ad word marketing program on Google, I plan on a certain level of return. If we invest $1,000, we have to generate not $1,000 in sales, but over $1,000 in net profit. In fact, I might expect to get back $1,500 in net profit. This is equivalent to expectations around return on a stock.

For example, if I am going to invest $1,000 in a 30 day pay-per-click ad word marketing program on Google, I plan on a certain level of return. As mentioned and illustrated in Figures 15.1 and 15.2, if we invest $1,000, we have to generate not $1,000 in sales, but over $1,000 in net profit. In fact, I might expect to get back $1,500 in net profit. This is equivalent to expectations around return on a stock.

With specific expectations in mind, you can track the performance of the program to see how it is doing and if it's meeting your net profit goals.

Each marketing program might have different horizons for monitoring. With pay-per-click, weekly monitoring is reasonable. Your Website might be monitored monthly, whereas direct mail might require a three-month window. The most important aspect of monitoring performance is doing it regularly. It should become part of your daily, weekly, or monthly review process.

The next critical aspect will be making a change. Looking at Figure 15.3, you can see that two stocks have exceeded expectations and two have underachieved. So, you're at a decision point. Should you continue investing in the underachieving stocks, or sell them and put the money into new stocks or the high performers?

Stock Name	Target Price	Actual	Performance
Apple	$175	$185	Winner
Google	$488	$475	Loser
GE	$58	$50	Loser
Microsoft	$74	$86	Winner

Figure 15.3

The same can be applied to your marketing program portfolio. Figure 15.4 illustrates various marketing programs.

Program Name	Expected Return	Actual Return	Performance
E-mail	25 leads	27 leads	Winner
Ad Words	10 conversions	18 conversions	Winner
Direct Mail	45 leads	5 leads	Loser
Print Ads	15 leads	2 leads	Loser

Figure 15.4

As you can see, e-mail and ad words are working great. Direct mail and print advertising, not as well, specifically when you consider the cost of each program. You could continue the latter two if you want to give them more time. However, a more prudent decision would be to cancel those programs and invest that money into e-mail and ad words to maximize the investment and return on marketing.

After you've worked with it, you'll find that ROMI is pretty straightforward. .

The payoff for figuring out your ROMI is the elimination of poor-performing marketing tactics, the understanding of how marketing makes you money, and a quantifiable approach to your marketing as opposed to hope and guesswork.

Start Today! Tips

1. Compute projected ROMI returns for the at least two marketing tactics you are considering.

2. Compute the ROMI for all your current marketing tactics and make "Winner" or "Loser" decisions for each of them.

3. Schedule a regular time to evaluate marketing programs, make decisions regarding marketing programs, and review investment requirements for your marketing.

▮ Chapter 16

THE INTERNET IS THE BEST THING SINCE...

A Marysville, Washington company called the Cookie Cutter Shop sells 700 different shapes of cookie cutters. So if you're looking to make moose-shaped cookies, they have it. An owl? A hammer? They have it.

Not long ago, this company, whose logo and location conjures up a little cabin off a dirt road deep in the woods, would have been limited to attracting customers within a 20-mile radius. After all, how far are people going to drive to buy a cookie cutter? To sell beyond that distance would have involved placing ads in national cooking magazines or creating a catalog and mailing it to potential customers – both very expensive options.

On top of being pricey, neither of those strategies was guaranteed to succeed. That's because both of them are passive in nature. Both depend on (a) the audience even *seeing* the ad or catalog – no guarantee in today's crowded media landscape – and (b) the person needing a cookie cutter at the exact moment they see the ad or catalog.

Today, there's a whole new set of marketing options for the owner of the Cookie Cutter Shop and most involve the Internet. As in, www.thecookiecuttershop.com.

The best part about the Internet is that using it to market your company is <u>much</u> cheaper than practically any other option. And <u>much</u> more effective. For example, first the owner of the Cookie Cutter Shop created a Website. Then she launched a simple and inexpensive "pay-per-click" advertising campaign through a search engine such as Google. Now, every time someone types in "cookie cutters" her shop comes up on the right side of Google (the sponsored links). And she only pays Google when someone actually clicks on her ad!

This means that people from all over America – not to mention the world – can now buy from the little Cookie Cutter Shop in the backwoods of Washington. In the past, the target market for the shop was extremely limited; now anyone, anywhere can purchase their products.

The cost of this campaign? As low as $50 a month.

We found out about the Cookie Cutter Shop because a friend of ours in Pennsylvania placed an order with this company via the Internet. He needed a cookie cutter in the shape of a cabin. He sat down at his computer, typed "cookie cutters" into Google and up came the shop. He clicked on the ad, was taken to the site and within five minutes had ordered four cabin-shaped cookie cutters for $16. And because the Cookie Cutter Shop owner is smart, she keeps a database of all of her visitors and customers and sends them regular e-mails letting them know about new products.

Ten years ago this just wouldn't (couldn't!) have happened. Our friend never would have known about the Cookie Cutter Shop and probably never would have found a cabin cookie cutter in any of his local stores.

Here are some reasons why your Website is your best marketing tool.

1. It's available to your prospects 24/7.
2. It's easily and instantly updated.
3. It reduces administrative efforts.

4. It communicates on a grand scale.
5. It slashes printing and distribution costs.
6. If you do it right, it tells your story in a way your prospects will understand.

And companies are wise to this; just about every major and minor corporation has one. In 2002, 35 percent of all businesses had Websites. By the end of 2006, that number had more than doubled to 85 percent! Today, it's probably closer to 100 percent. Yahoo reported that at the end of 2007, 88 percent of shoppers looked through a company's Website first. And that same holiday season, 80 percent of the visitors bought something online.

So the Website is the *keystone* to your entire marketing program. In the old days, a *keystone* was defined as a central wedge that locks the parts of an arch together. In the 21st century, however, the keystone or Website is the virtual "wedge" that holds together your Internet marketing program. Figure 16.1 illustrates the keystone concept.

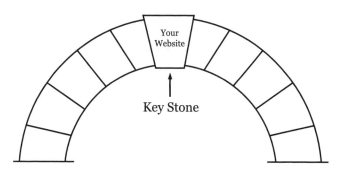

Figure 16.1

Thus, your Website should be the center of all your marketing activities. Your first thought at all times should be "put this on the Website," "feature this on the Website," and "let's update the Website."

However, the *Website* is one of four essential tools that make up an effective Internet marketing strategy. Along with *e-mail marketing,* which was discussed in earlier chapters and utilizes a database of contacts, the others – *a pay-per-click campaign,* and *search engine optimization (SEO)* – are equally important. Figure 16.2 illustrates their relationship and interaction with each other.

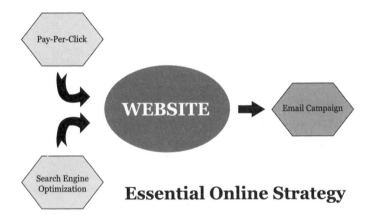

Essential Online Strategy

Figure 16.2

Thus your company can use the four essential prongs of an Internet marketing strategy:

- An effective Website
- E-mail marketing
- Pay-per-click
- Search engine optimization (SEO)

To further show how the elements of an effective Internet marketing strategy can work in tandem, let's look at our client, Pretzel Boy's.

Pretzel Boy's, the small chain of shops that sells Philadelphia-style soft pretzels, decided to offer franchises across the U.S. But the owner didn't know how to get the word out to potential franchisees. In the past, businesses wanting to franchise placed ads in local newspapers and national entrepreneurial magazines or hung signs in their store windows. Such marketing was basically ineffective; a passive, sluggish way of finding people who might be seriously interested in buying a franchise.

Our first suggestion was to create a <u>Website</u> that explained the benefits and requirements for being a Pretzel Boy's franchisee. Instead of focusing on how great the pretzels are —remember the red test/blue test from Chapter 6? – we discussed the advantages of owning a Pretzel Boy's shop and how wonderful a person's life would be if he or she owned one of these shops. Now prospective franchises visit the Website, learn about the company, and complete an online application to get the process started.

We also offered a free report—available in exchange for an e-mail address of course—with the stories of three successful Pretzel Boy's franchisees. We took those <u>e-mails and built a database of people</u> who visited the site.

To promote Pretzel Boy's Website, we created a $50-a-week <u>pay-per-click</u> campaign through Google. In the first week, the owner had 14 phone calls from people inquiring about a franchise. One of those 14 ended up buying a franchise for the $35,000 fee. Not a bad return on the initial marketing investment.

The other 13 people who weren't ready to make a decision stayed in the owner's database. Once the list got up to about 200, we started an e-mail campaign that reminded them of the benefits associated with franchise ownership, shared testimonials, and other possible profits. Each time this monthly e-mail went out, a few more people reignited their conversation with the owner and he sold more franchises.

The list below includes the Google Internet search terms used to attract potential franchisees to Pretzel Boy's.

- Philadelphia Soft Pretzel Franchise
- Soft Pretzel Franchise Bakery
- Buy Soft Pretzel Franchise
- Franchising Soft Pretzel Stores
- Philadelphia Pretzel Franchise

Once we achieved success on the "right side" of Google (the sponsored side), we tackled the left side (the free listings most people are familiar with).

We also utilized <u>search engine optimization (SEO) techniques</u>. Through adding key words to the content throughout the site as well as meta tags, image tags, strategic linking, and other tactics, we were able to provide a greater number of "hits" from people searching for franchise opportunities. Typically, search engines provide higher rankings when your content directly matches your search phrases.

Also, by testing key words and search terms in the pay-per-click campaign, Pretzel Boy's was able to identify the terms generating the most conversions. There's a good reason why so many organizations take SEO seriously: without the proper words and phrases, even the nicest-looking Websites fail to generate inquiries and sales.

To explain further, search engines constantly send "spiders" out across the Internet. These spiders look at millions of Websites on a daily basis for the words or phrases relevant to their users' searches. Pages that spiders recognize as containing the relevant words and content are recorded in their databases.

These databases—and not the Internet as a whole—is where the search engine looks each time someone starts a search. Links within these databases are ranked according to their relevancy to each specific search word or phrase. So it's essential that when spiders visit your site they easily find the key words and phrases that people most often use when searching. If spiders find plenty of these words on your site, you will rank highly in subsequent search results. That's why it is so important to focus on:

- Identifying appropriate key words and phrases.
- Making sure spiders can find them in your content.

With these objectives in mind, the *development of key words and phrases* for the site is crucial. This often means describing your products or services in a way that potential customers understand which might differ from your own corporate terminology.

Once you select key words and phrases that match your prospects' terminology and refer specifically to what they are looking for, make sure the site content incorporates them correctly. This is partly about ensuring that key words/phrases are included in appropriate places on each page. For example, most search engine "spiders" look at the headline and first paragraph of each page rather than a paragraph at the bottom. They also tend to look at the names of links, another good place to incorporate key words and phrases.

Finally, continue to monitor the site's search engine performance. This should be done monthly, at the very least, although weekly is probably better. The more closely you look at performance, the better equipped you'll be to make changes that will further improve search engine results.

With the essential tools in place, Pretzel Boy's is now able to sell few 2-3 franchises a month for an amazingly low investment.

Marketing through the Internet has many other advantages. In a sense, it's like a spigot – turn it on and you'll receive almost instantaneous feedback. In just one week and for only dollars a day, you'll know whether your strategy is working, which is almost completely opposite of traditional marketing. You can then open up the spigot and it will flow faster. If your program isn't working, you turn can it off quickly and try something else, like changing key words in your pay-per-click campaign.

The Internet – or to be more specific, its various search engines – has also created a new form of marketing called *reverse marketing*. In the past, companies had to publish an ad in a newspaper or magazine and hope that the target found the ad. Now, people with a need—"I need a cookie cutter in the shape of a pine tree right now!" — can proactively find the product or service at their leisure. Its *permission-based* marketing allows customers looking for your services to seek you out. Once they find you and sign up for your no-risk offer which should also be on your Website, they're giving you permission to continue the conversation. The beautiful aspect is that people come looking for you, as opposed to you searching for them.

Thus you can leverage the power of digital marketing tools and the Internet to create an entirely new source of leads – all for less investment than traditional methods. Not only does this drive down marketing expenses but it also increases your leads.

Reality Byte

Scratching Your Competitor's Back

What do tech titan IBM and Russell Roofing, a 50-person roofer in Oreland, Pa., have in common?

They're both happy to send valued customers elsewhere—even to a competitor—to deliver great service. Companies don't get a ticket to the Dow 30 without cultivating broad and deep networks of partners.

Russell Kaller's customers have plenty of needs too—like landscaping, electrical work, masonry, windows and on and on. Russ' company sells roofs. He doesn't have the skill or the bodies to handle all that other stuff. But he knows where to find people who do, and those referrals—especially from a trusted source—go a long way toward making customers happy.

How did Russ establish his partner network? Time helps; he's been in the roofing game for over 20 years. He works trade events, bumps into people on other jobs. In short, he shakes a lot of hands.

But Russ is picky, too. He only chooses established partners with conscientious owners and solid reputations. "I'd rather not recommend anyone at all than someone I can't trust to offer the same quality workmanship that I do," he says.

But going the extra mile for customers isn't just about partner referrals. Sometimes you have stump for the competition, too.

Russ isn't afraid to recommend competitors either. There's plenty of specialized roofing work he doesn't do, and plenty of geographical areas he can't adequately cover. There are also plenty of customers who just aren't the right fit (as in cheapskates who prefer aluminum-based materials over his recommended copper). So he's happy to shuttle those folks to a competitor where it makes sense—and he's even been known to ring up his rivals to compliment them on a job well done.

Unlike IBM, Russ doesn't have the time or resources to create formalized lead-generation agreements. And while he does track referrals received from partners and competitors, Russ doesn't keep records of—or, for that matter, charge for—leads he himself has generated. "It's not cost-effective to spend the time tracking commissions or finders fees," he says.

What's the payoff? "When I refer a fellow roofer a job, I almost always get a referral back in return," he says. Russ claims that more than 50% of his work comes from referrals—a big chunk of that from partners.

Bottom line, says Russ: "I'm a service provider to my customers." He's got that right.

Gene Marks CPA

The Marks Group PC - Author of *The Streetwise Small Business Book of Lists.* www.marksgroup.net

 # Start Today! Tips

1. Set up an account with Google Ad Words.

2. Create your list of key words and review your Website to make sure they are included appropriately and used often in the copy on your site.

3. Create a test ad, set a budget and test drive Google Ad Words. Set expectations and track results. Give it at least two weeks.

4. Perform the red/blue test of your Website. Make changes to ensure your site talks about how you can solve your clients' pains more than it talks about you.

5. Start a monthly e-mail campaign. There are a number of options but MyEmma (www.myemma.com) and iContact (icontact.com) works well for small businesses.

▌Chapter 17
MAKE YOUR WEBSITE WORK FOR YOU

These days, most businesses have Websites. They may not be slick and glitzy and may have been designed by the owner's teenaged nephew, but they have them nonetheless.

It goes without saying that if you don't have one yet, you should. However, your Website may be more about you and less about your prospects, customers, or clients. Apply the red/blue test discussed in Chapter 6 to see if this is the case. You may in fact need some enhancements so your site can work for you by facilitating sales and attracting prospects. It can do much of the heavy lifting of your marketing plan and become an active cog in your Marketing Machine™.

To accomplish this, however, your Website will need some additional critical components along with those discussed in previous chapters. Together, these factors will help ensure that visitors stick around long enough to learn how you can help them (hence, the term "sticky" when referring to successful Websites). They are as follows:

1. Headline with pain statement. This helps you connect with visitors instantly.
2. Solutions, linked to pain statement.
3. Empathetic photos.
4. E-mail capture mechanisms that provide no-risk and low-risk offers in exchange for e-mail address and or contact info from visitors.

5. No-risk offer associated with e-mail capture, making sure there is something for all your target markets.
6. Customer testimonials. These should be used liberally on the home page and throughout the site. People want to hear about others who share their pain.
7. Interactive elements. These can be videos, interactive quizzes, Podcasts, etc.

To make your site even "stickier" try adding these additional elements.

1. Free resources section. Include articles, stories, presentations, suggested books, archived e-newsletters and more.
2. Key differentiators. Clearly communicate what makes you remarkable, be bold and specific.
3. In the news. People want to see that your business is current, so post items that are interesting and relevant.
4. Events. If you host them, people will come. Promote workshops, Webinars, lunches, sponsorships, and any other activities on the site.

Two of our client's Websites illustrate the use of Reality Marketing™ and the Marketing Machine™. One offers parents of fussy children free downloads of stories which are read by a narrator. These stories are available online or via mobile devices, like a cell phone.

The initial focus of the site was on the story and the technical aspect of the download, rather than the issues faced by potential customers, as illustrated by Figure 17.1.

Figure 17.1

Figure 17.2 illustrates the incorporation of Reality Marketing.™ Along with graphic and visual upgrades, we utilized all of the recommended components to ensure that visitors quickly engage with the site, click around, and learn more. Most importantly, we provided contact information to help with the client's ongoing marketing effort.

Figure 17.2

Figure 17.3 shows implementation of the optional components.

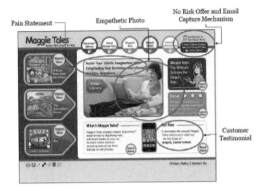

Figure 17.3

The next example is a company that provides benefits management services to CFOs and VPs of Human Resources at medium to larger size corporations.

Figure 17.4 shows the site before implementation of Reality Marketing ™ and Figure 17.5, after.

Figure 17.4

Figure 17.5

Figure 17.6 shows that, that in addition to the pain statements, empathetic photos, and a no-risk offer with e-mail capture mechanism, this site has two useful additional components.

- The "In The News" section allows the company to highlight new and interesting happenings. Events, like trade shows, workshops, or charitable activities can be publicized. Visitors see recent postings and understand the company is active, progressive, and current.
- A "Free Resources" section can educate prospective customers. Providing information to prospects is an excellent way to promote goodwill towards the company and get them thinking about how they can use its services.

Additionally, this site provides interactive tools that let prospects get involved with this firm. The Health Benefit Quiz and Cost Trend Modelers allow prospects to share vital information and in exchange, the company provides them with educational tools. All the while it collects contact data and sets the sales process into motion.

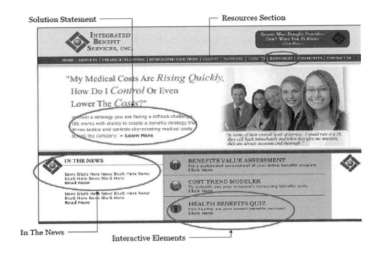

Figure 17.6

While the first example was a business to consumer (B2C) site, this is a business to business site (B2B). However, the motivators are the same and Figures 17.1-17.2 and 17.4-17.5 showed how the sites were transformed from electronic brochures that were "all about me" – that is, the businesses themselves – into marketing tools that addressed customers' pain and provided remarkable solutions.

Your Website should automate as many things as possible. Online scheduling, distribution of information, automated requests, lead referrals, virtual sample kits, online purchasing, and free downloads all contribute to easy access to on-demand information for clients and prospects. Figure 17.7 is an example of an automated lead referral program.

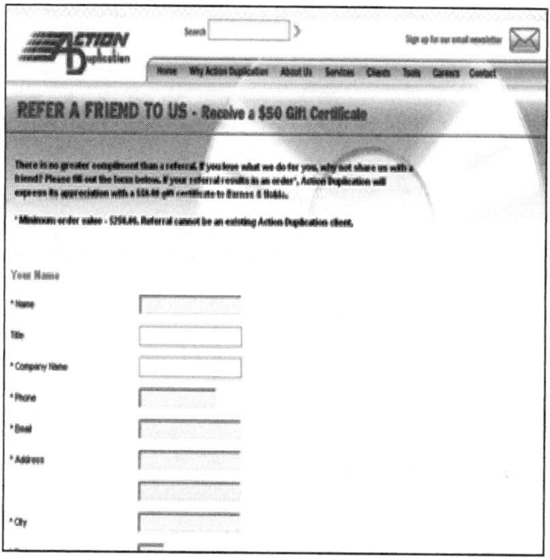

Figure 17.7

Finally, you need to monitor the performance of your Website. Track the numbers of first-time visitors coming to your site now and then track them after you make changes and implement marketing tactics. This will provide insight as to how your overall marketing is doing. You should expect weekly increases in the number of first-time visitors and page views.

 **Start Today! Tips**

1. Review your Website with a critical eye. Circle references to you in red and those to your clients in blue.

2. Go through your copy and make the changes so the site talks about prospects and clients, not you.

3. Make sure pain statements, coupled with the relevant solution, are prominently displayed on the home page.

4. Review your site to see what Reality Marketing™ components are missing. Plan to include those in your revised site.

5. To see a wide variety of sample Websites that use the Reality Marketing™ approach, visit www.square2marketing.com/portfolio-web.htm.

▎Chapter 18

PLANNING IS HALF THE BATTLE

If your marketing plan consists of one part wing and one part prayer you're not alone. In a recent survey, approximately 86 percent of businesses with less than $10 million in sales do not formally plan their marketing activities.

Instead, they ping-pong between unrelated tactics. Let's run newspaper ads! No wait, let's try a coupon book! How about a direct mailer? This rep just told me I should be on billboards!

There's no review of what has worked and what hasn't. And little if any thought has been given to an overall strategy.

Some real-world examples include signing up for a full-page ad in the Yellow Pages because the rep said "it would work;" deciding to "do some marketing" when business is slow but then dropping the campaign when a big order comes in; or listening to your brother-in-law who says radio ads are "the way to go."

These examples offer a *reactive* – and therefore very ineffective – approach to marketing. Why? Because they're not connected to a central strategy. They're schizophrenic. They provide no traction or forward motion, and result in wasted time and money.

You need to come up with a specific marketing plan, preferably one that covers a full year. When doing this, first consider *overall strategy*. Rather than planning what you'll be doing in January or April or October, plan what you're doing, period. For example, what messages do you want your prospects to receive? What makes you remarkable? What do you want the customer experience to be like? Do you have a system in place to ensure that every customer receives the same experience? What are the best ways to reach your customers – e-mail, direct mail, open houses, etc.? In other words, focus on the big picture.

Secondly, come up with a *calendar of marketing activities*. Exactly when will you put out that direct mail piece? When will you hold an open house? Should you run ads in the spring or fall? This involves literally taking out a calendar and penciling in when you are going to launch certain strategies.

It doesn't have to be fancy. In fact, it can be as simple as the sample marketing calendar in Figure 18.1.

The Marketing Planning Calendar™

2008 Marketing Events:	JAN	FEB	MAR	APR	MAY	JUN	JUL	AUG	SEP	OCT	NOV	DEC
1.												
2.												
3.												
4.												
5.												
6.												
7.												
8.												
9.												
10.												
11.												
12.												

Figure 18.1

Putting together a marketing calendar gives you something to look at every day and holds you accountable. It's documented and helps establish a marketing "rhythm." It also keeps you on track and helps avoid snap (and usually incorrect) decisions such as buying a full-page ad in the Yellow Pages (used by fewer people these days, thanks to the Internet).

The calendar also helps circumvent conflicts that may harm your marketing efforts. For example, it's probably a bad idea to plan an open house on Super Bowl Sunday or to market your business to accountants in April, the height of tax season. Calendar considerations include seasonal cycles, industry events, holidays, major competitor activity and important prospect or client events.

For example, Kool-Aid Heating and Air Conditioning uses seasonal marketing. Its advertising needs change drastically in the summer when everyone needs to get their air conditioning working and again in winter for heating. Kool-Aid can take advantage of its busiest months – June and October – by planning its ads and promotions well in advance. Because they know their peak parts of the year, they focus their advertising on seasonal needs and bring in maximum revenue. They also plan special promotions targeted to their busiest times.

For example, in March, well ahead of the busy air conditioning season, Kool-Aid runs ads offering a 20 percent discount on an AC tune-up. March is a fairly slow time for air conditioning companies. It does the same in September for the heating aspect of their business.

By planning ahead for the year, Kool-Aid knows exactly what it will be doing in March and September, as well as all the other months of the year. A plan like this helps keep companies on track and away from the ineffective "ping pong" strategy.

Getting started is easy. All you need to do is pull out a piece of paper and sketch out a rough marketing plan for the year. You don't even have to do everything you write down. Even if you only accomplish most of what you put on paper you'll be ahead of where you were without a plan.

Follows are some examples of programs for your marketing planning calendar:

- Plan an event, like an open house
- Website promotion, like a contest
- Make regular telemarketing phone calls
- Create and send electronic brochures
- Send out direct mail, like a postcard
- Produce a quarterly newsletter
- Go to an industry trade show
- Tap your current clients for new prospects
- Get an article in your local paper
- Ask your customers what they want via a survey
- Educational workshop, like Webinars, Podcasts, and workshops

To fund your proposed marketing strategies, you'll need to figure out how much to spend. There are four ways to set a marketing budget:

1. **Percentage of sales.** This is probably one of the most popular methods and usually ranges from 1-20 percent of a company's annual budget. The allocation increases (or decreases) with the sales revenue of the company and will never spin out of control or deplete sales revenue.
2. **Dollar approach.** This method involves setting a hard dollar amount, say $25,000, for the year. While relatively easy, it involves making an estimate with no comparative past results.
3. **Matching competitors.** This method is simple and will keep you in line with others in your field. But it involves

guesswork and assumes the competition is spending the correct amount.

4. **Marketing plan objectives.** This is the Reality Marketing™ method and is the most effective. It is quite involved and requires using your marketing objectives to determine the budget and estimating the expenditure you'll need to achieve your marketing objectives. For example, if you need $34,680 to execute your plan, then that's your budget.

The planning process is one of the many components of an effective marketing program. However, a planned marketing program will beat the pants off of an unplanned effort any day of the week.

 Start Today! Tips

1. Using your calendar, contact vendors to determine the exact costs of the marketing tactics you want to accomplish.

2. Identify opportunities on the calendar (seasons or events) that you can leverage into the various programs listed in this chapter.

3. Create a marketing team in your company to help execute the calendar of events.

▍Chapter 19

HOW DOES MARKETING IMPACT SALES?

How does a Marketing Machine™ that's pumping out leads on a daily basis mesh with the sales process? The sales process and the Marketing Machine™ need to work together in an integrated fashion, so leads are taken through a system to produce revenue.

For example, after evaluating six months of work, a client decided that their marketing <u>still</u> wasn't working. When we asked them how they measured the program's effectiveness, they replied, "We've invested all this time and money and haven't·seen sales grow."

Yet this particular client had enjoyed increased business activity in terms of generating leads so we decided to dig further. Because each component of their Marketing Machine™ can be tracked, it was easy to compile a report on the number of leads generated. We simply reviewed the baseline activity of lead flow from the beginning of the marketing effort until now.

The company averaged 20 opportunities a month prior to building the Marketing Machine™. Now they were averaging around 115 opportunities per month. Obviously there's a disconnect if you're getting over five times the amount of leads yet sales are not rising in proportion.

Upon further investigation, we realized that the sales department lacked a defined strategy. Along with needing training in the product itself and a better (and therefore more motivating) compensation plan, the four sales representatives lacked defined territories as well as a lead distribution strategy. They simply answered phone and in-person queries, gave prices, and offered volume discounts.   There was no procedure for handling new customers or leads. No wonder sales remained stagnant!

It's not enough to get people to go to your Website and fill out a form or make a phone call into your company. It's crucial that your sales team respond in a defined and strategic fashion, so that you close as many of those golden leads as quickly and efficiently as possible.

For your company to be remarkable, it also needs to be outstanding in its initial sales contacts with prospects. So your sales strategy should also always consider the customer first. Ultimately, you want to guide them through a process that provides all the answers to their questions and takes them towards the end result – a sale.

An effective sales process has three parts – mapping, tracking, and managing. To begin, you *map out* what happens when someone says, "I would like to take the next step with your company." Figure 19.1 illustrates a sample sales process map.

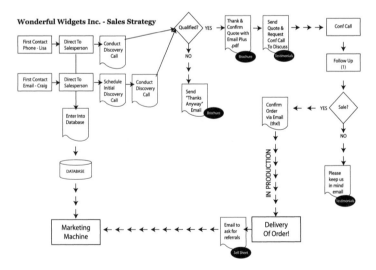

Figure 19.1

In this map, there are many places for "yes" and "no" decisions. These are crucial in eliminating unqualified leads. Say a lead comes to your company and then wants to take the next step. Immediately, you schedule a 30-minute "discovery call" for a free consultation with your company. However, those 30-minute calls can also be used to ask pertinent questions and make sure the lead is a qualified customer. Questions could include the following:

1. How does your decision-making process work?
2. Who is the ultimate decision maker for this purchase? Make sure you're talking to the decision-maker. You could spend weeks or even months discussing the product or service with someone with no purchase authority, only to find out you have to start all over again with their boss.
3. What business goals or objectives are you trying to attain as a result of working with us?
4. Have you hired a firm or purchased products/services like this in the past?
5. What are your requirements for working with a firm like mine?
6. How much money have you budgeted for this purchase?

For more questions, visit www.realitymarketingrevolution.com.

These and other questions should be asked during the initial qualification call to ensure that this prospect is worth taking to the next step. Although in some instances prospects may not qualify, with the Marketing Machine™, we keep talking to them in case their situation might change. You never know when their pain will become acute and they turn out to be the perfect prospect.

If they are qualified, you take them to the next step, which in Figure 19.1 is a face-to-face meeting. The client is a provider of consulting services, so the average sale is approximately $30,000. Prospects are looking for a partnership, not just a transaction so they want to get to know the salesperson and company before doing business with them. Any sales process needs to support this "get to know you" approach.

Now that you have a map that shows exactly how prospects will flow through your sales process, you need to *track* how they make their purchase decision. Tracking is crucial since timing is vital to the sales process, with pauses (for decision-making) and follow-ups as appropriate. Transactional sales might require immediate follow-up, but the consulting clients need more time. They want to schedule the 30-minute discovery call at least two or three days out, for several reasons:

1. They don't want to appear desperate for business.
2. They want a chance to review the prospect's Website, organize their initial thoughts, do competitive research, and be prepared with some intelligent insights.
3. They want to send the prospect an informational package in the mail for review before the call.

If you provide a proposal to the client and indicate to them that you will be calling them in two days, after they've had a chance to review and talk among their management team, then the tracking system in your Marketing Machine™ will automatically remind you when it's time to follow up. The point of your marketing effort is to drive lots of leads, and you need to effectively manage them in an organized fashion. So it's vital to get back to them in the appropriate amount of time, whether it's within the hour to follow up on a transactional purchase or several days for a longer-range decision, like the consulting services. Waiting too long or rushing the process is counterproductive and will only lose sales to the competition. Tracking eliminates most of these problems.

Finally, you need to *manage* the sales process; that is, make sure that the sales department acts consistently in their dealings with every prospect. Everyone needs to be providing information and handling leads in the same fashion. Managing should also be done regularly, such as having a review once a week, which we found to be effective in our own company, or through a morning "sales huddle" to discuss what's going on for the day. You can decide what's appropriate to make sure that the level and amount of communication matches the needs of your business. Such reviews provide an opportunity to evaluate all leads and ensure that everything possible is being done to close the sale.

Start Today! Tips

1. Map out your company's sales process.

2. If you have sales people, investigate sales training options in your area.

3. Start to track leads, proposals, and closed deals.

4. Interview lost deals to improve your "pitch."

Chapter 20
PIPELINE, PIPELINE, PIPELINE

You know what they say about real estate – location, location, location. Well, the same is true of sales, except that it's pipeline, pipeline, pipeline.

What exactly is a sales pipeline? Basically it consists of the prospective clients in the suspect, prospect, or lead phases of your marketing efforts. Following are some samples of how this works.

Don! How are we doing this month?
> *Great Jim, my pipeline has never been better.*

Don! Is Company Y going to close today?
> *I don't know Jim, but it doesn't even matter, because my pipeline is so strong, I have three more just like them ready to close too.*

Mary, how does next quarter look?
> *Great Jim, my pipeline is so good; we have all the opportunities we need to hit our numbers.*

Jim, Company X wants a discount of 20 percent to close. Can I give it to them?
> *What does your pipeline look like? Well, it looks great. Then let's hold true on our pricing and keep our profit margin intact.*

You may have had the experience of asking your sales team for projections on what business will close before the end of the month and getting blank stares. It's probably because your company lacks a rating system to score prospective deals; the reps have no idea of the strength or weakness of the sales pipeline. Along with providing a forward view of the health of your sales projections and its overall strength in general, a good pipeline will rate both individual and overall opportunities.

Sales people, being positive and enthusiastic by nature, will always view the chances of closing a new client much greater than the likely reality. So there needs to a quantifiable rating system that's objective, easy-to-use and enables management to look forward in sales projection.

An effective and simple way to establish a pipeline is the *"Pain, Authority, Match" (PAM)* methodology. Basically, it involves assigning a numeric score from 0-5 in the three categories for every prospect in the pipeline. These scores are fluid and dynamic and as the salesperson works the opportunity, they should improve. The closer you get to the opportunity for closing, the higher the score.

Pain

The first qualification is *Pain*. Is the company or individual facing serious enough issues that they need a solution to their problem? For example, a 10-person IT service and computer hardware provider has a potential client whose computer network crashes on a weekly basis. It's impossible for them to do business unless the situation is fixed quickly. Their "pain" is acute. If they don't get this resolved, they might actually go out of business.

Another example is a client who is planning a company-wide printer upgrade from black-and-white inkjets to color lasers. It's a nice-sized order, but nothing that needs to be done today. While they have pain, it's not mission critical. Even if their upgrade took a month, business would go on as it has for the past year.

The opportunity to land the job to reconfigure a broken network is much greater and could happen much faster given the increased amount of pain. The chance to upgrade the printer network that's already working is also a good one, but it's going to take longer and might be more competitive. So in a situation like this, the opportunity with the crashing computer network would receive a "Pain" score of 4 or 5, but the upgrade printer network would be rated as a 1 or 2.

Authority

The next measure of qualification is *Authority*. Authority simply means the person you are talking to or working with has the authority to sign your contract, order, agreement, etc. They have the ability to create the budget required to secure your services and don't need to discuss it with anyone else. They alone have the power to say "yes."

How many times has your salesperson gone to an employee of the target company, pitched it, gotten great feedback, and then the deal never reaches the deciding executive? The project languishes in the pipeline because the salesperson is depending on their contact to deliver the story to the final decision-maker. While the contact may have the available budget, the decision-maker – the true power – has the ability to create the budget.

So once again, using the 0-5 scoring system, if you're selling a product and were talking directly to the business owner, then the rating would be a 5. If you're talking to the spouse of the business owner and he or she is working with the business owner to make the decisions, you might rank that a 4.

However, if you're talking to a manager in a large corporation and can't clearly define who is involved in the decision-making process, the authority rating might be a mere 1 or 2. For sales in general, determining the decision-maker goes a very long way in expediting or closing the sale.

Match

Match is another gauge as to whether your services or products are a good fit with the prospect company. For example, if the small IT firm gets from a call from a Fortune 500 company looking for bids on 900 new workstations to be installed in the next 60 days, it's likely a bad fit. They lack the resources to fill such a large sales request so quickly. If they receive an inquiry from a graphics design firm that only uses Macs and they specialize in PCs, they might be able to figure it out eventually, but a good match? Not so much. However, if a small-to-medium sized company comes to them looking for a specialized computer system similar to what they've previously implemented for several satisfied clients, then it's a great match.

Using our scoring system, if something is a perfect match and the company adopts your program or service without breaking stride, it would rate a 4 or 5. If the product or service you're recommending is not quite a fit, a 2 or 3 might be a reasonable score.

Now use PAM to help project your sales. Go through your list of potential clients and rate the PAM of each one, adding up the total of the three scores. Say you rank pain as a 4, authority as a 3, match a 2. In this scenario, the total score is 9 out of 15 possible points. Not the greatest opportunity, but one that might turn into a sale, with a little work.

In another example pain gets a 5; authority, 5; and match, 4. Now, the total score is 14 out of 15 and the chances of closing the sale soon and quickly are much higher.

Figure 20.1 illustrates how to measure the health of your pipeline by taking the examples one step further. If you know that the deal has a rating of 12 out of a possible 15 use Figure 20.1 to see when you can expect this to close.

Pain, Authority, Match Score	Expected Close
13 to 15	within 30 days
10 to 12	within 60 days
7 to 9	within 90 days
under 7	not qualified enough to project

Figure 20.1

Gaining access to authority, proving your match, and helping the client understand the severity of their pain actually improves the PAM score and moves the prospect more quickly through the sales cycle to a close.

Managers can help their sales teams work their prospects through the system. The system also provides an easy way for salespeople to develop a consistent vocabulary when doing forecasting and assists them in understanding how to project sales for the future month or quarter. The point is to take the guesswork out of the pipeline!

Start Today! Tips

1. Consider implementing a sales tracking system if you don't already have one. Also create a list of your sales opportunities, including the names of all the potential prospects you or anyone on your team are working on.

2. Take the PAM system and score each of the opportunities. This will give you a much clearer idea of how to project revenue over the next 30, 60, or 90 days. It will also provide a standard vocabulary for talking about opportunities with your sales team.

3. Keep track of the PAM score of your opportunities. For example, if you talk to a prospect and they move from a possibility to a viable customer, update your score. Now you have a real-time system to measure the actual potential of your sales efforts.

Chapter 21
MAKING SURE YOU CLOSE THE SALE

Many companies barrage prospects with follow-up phone calls, e-mails, faxes, and special requests to try to get them to close. So it's up to you to analyze what's appropriate for your company in luring these prospects. Leads are just an individual or company who says they are interested in doing business. You have to take them the rest of the way.

Unfortunately, too many situations of "not doing the right thing" have resulted in a lost sale. It has happened to us as well, when two companies approached us about coming together to form one new entity. They were looking for a new name, branding effort, and way to generate more customers to take advantage of their union.

Our business development person had taken them through the sales prospect perfectly and even had gotten to the closing point. When doing the final paperwork, the business development person realized that the prospect, which had a name, but no logo, had neglected to register their Website or URL address for the newly named company.

Since it is relatively affordable to register a name, and the chances of losing the perfect URL were great, the business development person asked our interactive manager to register the URL to make sure that it was secure. He also e-mailed the president of the prospective company, saying, "I also registered your name, and will drop you an invoice to get reimbursed for the $45 fee."

Well, the deal exploded in that very moment. While the business development person thought that he was doing the prospect a favor (the reason we say "prospect" is because the deal had not closed yet), the prospect viewed this as an aggressive move made by the company without its permission. The deal was dead.

Unwittingly, the business development person overstepped his bounds and made an assumption which caused the deal to crash and burn. He should have checked with us first, and we would have run it by the client. So as business owner, you need to clearly communicate the boundaries and levels of communication throughout your organization, whether it's a sales division, business development team, or customer service department. And knowing how to close the sale – and making sure your representatives can do so as well – is just as important as generating the initial lead.

Start Today! Tips

1. Take time and map out your current sales process. Be specific and make notes when you call, e-mail, or visit prospects in person. How many times do you follow up? What documents do you send them and when? This will help you see where improvements can be made.

2. Share your new sales process map with others in the company. Get feedback from prospects and members of your sales team to help make improvements, changes, or eliminate steps that delay sales or confuse the prospect.

3. After you are happy with the new process, share it with the entire company and especially the sales team. Let everyone know this is the new procedure to be followed by everyone involved.

4. No process is final, so continue to monitor your team to make sure it's implemented correctly and see if you can improve and refine it. Share any changes with your team.

Chapter 22
HOW DOES IT REALLY WORK?

In this chapter, we'll bring together Reality Marketing™ principles and strategies and provide a taste of what it's like to go through a real-life marketing challenge as experienced by "Tom Kramer" (not his real name), CEO of Select IT, whose Philadelphia-based company provides information technology services to small and medium-size businesses. Tom and his staff help clients with their computer hardware and software needs and develop their networks, provide protection for their systems and support for data backup plans, and use technology to enhance their business processes. The company's revenue was $3.4 million in 2006 but Tom's goal was to meet or exceed the $5 million mark by the end of 2007. Tom's first-person story illustrates how an effective marketing program can make a positive impact on you and your business.

Day 1 – March 15th
What a lousy day. Our biggest customer just gave me notice that he will be leaving us in a month. That accounts for almost 10 percent of my sales. I'm not quite sure how we're going to replace that business.

My dad started the company 18 years ago. I never really focused on sales or marketing to bring in new business. People just found us. And, to be perfectly honest, I hoped that the phone would ring when we were slow, and most of the time it did. Even when the calls didn't come in it always seemed to work out somehow.

However, I think the time has come to try and take this business to the next level, since "hoping" hardly seems to be the ticket to a successful future. Competition in my field is increasing, and with my kids going to college in a few years, my financial pressures are growing.

After lunch today, I'm going to do some initial research. Do I need a company to help me? Should I hire someone internally? Can I do this myself? Maybe read a book or two? Is it an advertising agency that I'm looking for? Since I'm new at this, I guess the Internet would be the best place to start.

I don't know what phrase to type into the search bar, so let's start with "marketing." Yikes, there are so many different listings! How about "marketing help" and since I would prefer to work with someone locally, I'll even refine it more by saying "marketing help Philadelphia." Let's see what comes up now.

Wow, still a lot of choices and they all look the same. But wait, here's one company that's providing free resources that might be helpful.

The ad says:

Need New Marketing?
Make marketing work for your business! Find free advice here.
www.square2marketing.com

Let me click through to their Website and see if any articles can get me thinking in the right direction. Hmmm, this site is interesting and it certainly sounds relevant because it talks about the problem I'm having as an entrepreneur: "How do I get my marketing working so that I can get more sales?"

But hold on a minute.... Before I enter the "Free Resources" section and get access to those articles, I have to give them my e-mail address. Should I do it? It seems a little risky because they might start spamming me. But I really need the help and we haven't had many new prospects call lately so I'll take the chance. At worst I can block them from my e-mail list if they starting bombarding me. At best, I get some free marketing help.

Wow, the "Free Resources" section has a <u>lot</u> of information. There are articles, suggested books, videos, Podcasts, and the company's blog. I can sign up for a free "lunch and learn" and listen to marketing ideas that have to do with the Internet. And they even offer a free coaching session.

I think I've found the place to start learning how to improve my company's marketing efforts. Let me download a few articles and see if I can help myself and find out about different ways to bring in new customers.

Day 5 – March 20

What a great day! I got a referral from an existing customer for a project that could turn out to be pretty big. Turns out I don't need any marketing after all. It was just a little slow period and it got me worried. I'm back in the game!

Day 11 – March 26

Well, the referral prospect call last week turned out to be nothing. She had no budget and now I feel worse than ever because I wasted so much time ignoring the real issues. Let me go back to that marketing Website and see if there's anything else I can use to help me.

Well, here's something new. Now they're offering a free workshop called "My Marketing Isn't Working and I Don't Know Why?!?" Does that sound like me, or what? Let me sign up. Hopefully there aren't any strings attached.

I just got the workshop confirmation and it seems on the up-and-up. The itinerary really strikes home: How to get new sales; how to change the way I think about marketing; and how to create a "machine" that automatically generates leads. This might be very helpful!

Day 26 – April 10
Well, the day of the workshop is finally here. Even though there was a semi-emergency in the office, this is too important to miss. I am really looking forward to getting some ideas on how to improve my marketing.

 **Reality Byte**

Are You Doing Time or Doing a Task?

Do you accomplish things based on what you have to get done (Task) or based on the time that you have to complete them? (Time). I never really thought about this much until a friend of mine moved from the city to a farm. She told me that where she would consider a task complete based on the time that she had when she was in the city, now, at the farm, she works at a task until it is complete.

This got me thinking…if I had more time to complete a task would I do it better? Do I do a task until it is really complete or good enough based on the time that I have? When we bought a beach house last year without cell or internet access, I found doing work around the house took longer to complete and I actually enjoyed it more! Without the time limit to get something complete, I could do it for however long I liked and to the level of completeness I wanted to. In the end, it felt a lot more relaxing and fulfilling.

In addition, I could truly strive for minimal achievement- by focusing on the task at hand only without all the other multi-tasking distractions. How much are you able to focus on task rather than time?

Barry Moltz
Entrepreneur, business consultant and author of *Bounce! The Path to True Business Confidence*
http://barrymoltz.com/blog

My goodness, there are 75 people at this workshop who sound just like me! They are all trying to get their small or medium-sized business to be a medium or large-sized business. The presenters had lots of good ideas and they even passed out a free workbook! I can't wait to get started.

Day 39 – April 23

It's two weeks later and that workbook is still sitting on the corner of my desk! I can't seem to find any time to devote to marketing and even if I did, I'm not quite sure exactly were to start.

Every week I get an e-mail from the company that put on the workshop. They provide some good tips, but I just don't have the time to act on them. I don't have anyone on staff who could help either. All of my employees are already busy with clients and keeping the business going. I think I'm going to sign up for a free consultation offered by the marketing company. It might be interesting to talk with someone about my business.

Day 45 – April 29
The consultation was much different than I anticipated. It wasn't about what this company can do for me. It was <u>all about me</u>. They asked me five key questions:

1. What is my revenue now and where do I want to be?
2. Who is my target market and who do I want to sell to in the future?
3. What problems, challenges, or "pains" do those prospects have when purchasing a product or service like mine?
4. What solutions does my company offer that solves those pains?
5. What makes my company so remarkable that people will choose or recommend me above and beyond my competitors? (that was the toughest to answer)

Those five questions got me thinking about my business. They made me realize that I need a strong marketing strategy. My options are to create one myself or hire someone to help me do it. Given my track record of trying to do this myself, the second option sounds like a much better approach.

I think I'm going to use this marketing company to help me do this right. That way, I set myself apart from the competition and hopefully people will start talking about my company and how we do things a little bit differently (and then spend a lot of money on our services). I think I'm ready to make a commitment to marketing and I think I found the partner who will help me reach my goal of $5 million in sales.

Day 47 – May 1

We just lost another major client – thank goodness I have engaged the services of this marketing company! My competition – an upstart in my area – has been attempting to lure my clients away from me, and this time they succeeded. To be perfectly honest, I have no prospects in the pipeline that could fill that revenue void and I'm very worried about the future of my business.

Day 48 – May 2

I've committed to a "whiteboard session," a half-day strategic messaging development session designed to help me figure out exactly who I want to be selling to, what their pains are, how to solve those pains, and what makes my business special. Although business is bad right now, I am looking forward to working with someone on strategic issues. I almost never get time to do that. I'm also excited about any new business opportunities that will come about because of this session. I wish it were tomorrow, instead of May 10th!

Day 56 – May 10

Well, the day has finally arrived for my strategic messaging "whiteboard" session. My controller and my lead salesperson will be joining me as well. I am going to the session not quite knowing what to expect, but understanding that we need to be open to change and willing to move out of our comfort zone to get what we want – a robust pipeline of new opportunities.

An entire team of people was on hand to help. We were assigned a dedicated marketing consultant to coach and counsel us with our marketing. And the firm partners even participated.

In the session, the ideas came fast and furious. What if we offered 24-hour service? What if we offered computer loaners? What if our vans were moving workshops? What if we provide instant diagnostic tools? Or proactive alerts before issues became problems?

I was surprised that with a few simple changes we could really do some wonderful things in the marketplace. The marketing company walked us through a process that allowed us to see our business through the eyes of our clients. I appreciated the objectivity and the introduction of new ideas and concepts.

Here are five "remarkable" new aspects of our business that we will talk about in our marketing:

- OneCall™ – Any time of the day or night, live access to our team for help with your technology issues.
- 59 or Free – Service tech is dispatched to your office in under 59 minutes or the service call is free.
- MyNetwork™ - A Web-based dashboard with details on the performance of your network, custom reports, and recommendations on how to improve performance, updated daily.
- Ask the Expert – online access to our team for instant inquiries and responses.
- Instant Alerts™ - proactive e-mail and text message alerts in advance of any critical issues.

I'm excited to take the company to the next level!

Day 64 – May 18

About a week after the in-person session I received a detailed Strategic Messaging Plan. Basically, it was mini-marketing plan that answered all of my questions, going back to when I originally contacted the marketing company.

Who should I be selling to? What are their problems, in their own terms? How do I solve those problems for them? Why am I different? Where should I spend my precious marketing dollars? All those questions were answered in a clear, concise strategy that would take me through the next 12 months.

Yes, I'm going to have to spend money to change some things, and yes, I'm going to have to commit time to making these improvements, but I think it's well worth it if I want my company to thrive and grow. This is the best possible decision for my company and its future.

Day 66 – May 20

After reviewing my new Strategic Messaging Plan/mini-marketing plan, I agreed on the eight marketing tactics required to achieve my goals. These projects will help me locate the prospects that I want to talk to and incrementally build my long-term marketing program.

The projects we will execute are as follows:

1. As a technology company, it's critical to create a stronger, more local online presence. We'll do this by identifying key messages and technology to showcase Select IT as a leader in the computer consulting via custom Website development and the inclusion of important marketing components.

2. In exchange for contact information and to build the prospect database, we will develop a series of informational and helpful white papers or no-risk offers.

3. We will teach the sales team to more effectively communicate what makes SelectIT special. This means creating, producing, and distributing electronic brochures and sell sheets.

4. We'll design a monthly e-mail campaign to keep clients and prospects in touch with SelectIT. This regular and rhythmic communication tactic will continue to sell, without our needing to use the sales force. It will also drive visitors to our newly created Website.

5. We'll send new visitors to the new SelectIT Website. Pay-per-click advertising programs through Google Ad Words and natural search engine optimization lets prospects easily find SelectIT and contributes to building a robust prospect database.

6. Addition of direct mail to the marketing mix will continue to communicate with prospects via more traditional direct marketing tactics.

7. To continue educating and attracting prospects, we'll create a Webcast, a "lunch and learn" or an educational workshop – or all three – to support ongoing low-risk offers.

8. We'll create a public relations program to generate interest through targeted media placements and press releases posted to the new Website—all talking about our new "remarkable" offerings.

Day 73 – May 27

Now that we have all of our tactics in place, we need to develop a rhythm to implement them. On the suggestion of the marketing company, I decided to establish a schedule of meetings. First, our management team will get together every Friday for fifteen minutes to review everyone's work. Here we can discuss weekly progress in marketing as well as overall advancement toward our longer-term goal of improving sales. Second, every morning from 9:15 to 9:20, we'll have a five-minute "huddle" with key management team members. This way, everybody is held accountable in accomplishing their daily marketing tasks, further ensuring that we can get to our ultimate goal by the end of the year.

Day 122 – July 15

It's been about six weeks since we signed off on our marketing program and started implementing the key tactics. Our new Website is finished and traffic is up 25 percent with more unique visitors and more page views. Better yet, fourteen people filled out the form saying that they were interested in starting a conversation with us. With that kind of activity, I'm actually thinking about hiring an additional salesperson.

Our prospect database(which started at around 400) is now up over 800, with each e-mail driving more activity. Even though we are only on our second monthly e-mail, the initial response has been overwhelmingly positive. I know I have to be patient to see a real sales impact, but we are moving in the right direction.

Day 272 – December 15

It's been six months since we started implementing the marketing changes . We've had much success in landing new clients and introducing new people to our business.

All we did is follow the step-by-step plans that the marketing company gave us and implemented it consistently throughout the entire time. As a result, marketing has really started to blossom.

# Reality Byte

The 5 Immutable Laws of Persuasive Blogging

Blogging is a great way to grow a business, promote a cause, or spread new ideas, because when you take an educational approach to marketing, you gain the attention and trust of people who might otherwise simply ignore old-fashioned advertising. Not only can those people become your customers or converts, they can also become your advocates.

While there are as many ways to approach blogging as there are blogs, some things remain steadfast when it comes to gaining influence and prompting action. Here are the 5 bedrock elements to keep in mind when you blog to persuade:

1. **The Law of Value**
   Your blog must provide value to the reader by addressing a problem, concern, desire, or need that the reader already has. Fresh, original content is critical.

2. **The Law of Headlines and Hooks**
   Your post titles must stand out in a crowded, noisy blogosphere, and you must quickly communicate the value of reading further with your opening.

3. **The Law of "How To"**
   People don't want to know "what" you can do, they want to know "how" it's done. If you think you're giving away too much information, you're on the right track.

4. **The Law of the List**
   Love them or hate them, informational posts presented in list format are easily digestible, and allow for an efficient transfer of your value proposition to the reader.

5. The Law of the Story

Stories are the most persuasive blogging element of all, as they allow you to present a problem, the solution, and the results, all while the connotation of the story allows readers to sell themselves on what you have to offer.

by Brian Clark
Copy Blogger
For more information and tips,
go to www.copyblogger.com

I know things are working because this week several clients came to us from different sources. Not just from referrals as had been done in the past, but instead from our Internet marketing program. Some also responded to our direct mail, while others found our e-mail newsletter valuable. Still others picked up the phone and called us after they'd received a few e-mails.

I've come to the conclusion that marketing tactics are like stocks in a portfolio. It's too risky to have just one stock. A more balanced, managed, and monitored approach allows you to make adjustments and watch your investment grow, just like we did with our marketing.

Day 302 – January 15

One of the key things about our new marketing programs is that we have been tracking and testing them all along to make sure that we don't waste any money on costly mistakes.

What we found was that programs we initially thought would work and what actually did work were completely different. By tracking these programs we can see, down to the penny, exactly how effectively we're spending our advertising dollars.

Initially we thought direct mail would be the best, because that's what we were most familiar with. But it's really been the e-mail marketing, search engine optimization, pay-per-click and the Website enhancements that have been leading in our return on marketing investment.

I used to dismiss the Website as just an online brochure. Now I see it as the centerpiece of the entire marketing program. I am actually thinking about adding some new pages and features to make it even more dynamic.

Day 362 – March 15

I'm now nearly at the end of the first year and can't believe the difference in the company. There is now much more prospecting and sales activity, and therefore more referrals. It also seems like much more of a team effort, since we're all working together with a single coordinated marketing program. I couldn't be more pleased with the changes.

I knew I had to move out of my comfort zone, but never anticipated this much success from a marketing program. SelectIT is well on its way to earning $5 million this year and perhaps even exceed that goal.

▌Conclusion

A HAPPY ENDING FOR THE ENTREPRENEUR

If you've ever seen a Broadway musical, you know that most of them end with the "Big Number." It's the high-energy song and dance that sends people out the theater doors tapping their toes and humming a tune.

Well, it's time for an inspiring send-off to get you revved up to go out and change the way you market your company.

Consider the benefits of making the changes outlined in this book:

Freedom. You will gain new freedom to work on large projects, do strategic planning, and be a leader. In short, you'll start to feel more like the *owner* of your business rather than being owned by it. This freedom will enable you to think bigger and more flexibly so that you can achieve the goals that you want.

What happens if you have more than enough business? No problem. You have the freedom to turn off the spigot and the number of leads will plateau and you can have exactly the size and kind of activity that you desire.

Satisfaction. Nothing beats the satisfaction that comes from starting a business and then seeing it grow and prosper. If you follow our advice you'll taste that success. You'll also find personal satisfaction. Once you get your Marketing

Machine™ up and running and your business starts taking off you can devote more time to what's most important to you – family, friends and an incredible work/life balance.

Financial success. If you're like most business owners, you work extremely hard at what you do. You should reap the financial rewards. Implementing the strategies talked about in this book will help you grow your business and take it to the next level.

Cash out. When you have a company that runs smoothly and has an automated system of driving new business, it becomes quite sellable. While this may not be your end goal, just think how much more your business is worth if you could walk away from the day-to-day operations and it would still generate the kind of profit that you enjoy today.

So, where to begin? How do you take the excitement we hope that you've gotten from reading this book and sustain it?

Stop leaving marketing and sales on the back burner and get serious.

Move out of your comfort zone and start putting the programs and strategies we have offered you into place.

Let yourself dream a little.

Grab a calendar and block out some time to get away from the office and work on your marketing.

Let yourself be creative and position yourself for new markets and more prospects.

Dedicate yourself to a new way of thinking about your business.

Marketing enables you to drive more people to your company, but if you're not dedicated to tightening up the systems and building a Marketing Machine™, don't spend a dime on additional advertising, because it's just going to be for naught.

Plan in advance, it's half the battle. Most marketing programs in small businesses are reactive. Be proactive. If it's February, you should know what you're going to be doing this summer.

To paraphrase Confucius, "every long journey begins with one small step." By buying and taking the information in this book to heart, you've accepted some of the things that make us a little bit different as entrepreneurs.

Consider the case of a Reality Marketing™ poster child, Rittenhouse Builders. Within 18 months of coming to us, the two owners – excellent construction and engineering professionals who didn't know a thing about marketing – had accepted every one of the principles you've read about in this book.

A few years later, we encountered one of the owners at a networking event. He pulled us aside to tell us that he had never really thanked us for what we had done to help his company and that he owed us a deep debt of gratitude for changing the way he did business. He told us that he is now living the life he wanted, still working hard, but doing it on the kinds of projects he's always dreamed about.

We love such stories because we know that not only have we given them the way to make more sales but a way to live a better life.

So get started today and take your first step on the journey to building your dream company.

And never say "My marketing isn't working and I don't know why?!?" ever again.

 Resources

REALITY MARKETING REVOLUTION RESOURCES
FOR SMALL TO MEDIUM SIZED BUSINESSES

ONLINE RESOURCES

American Express OPEN
www.open.com
> American Express OPEN is dedicated exclusively to the success
> of small business owners and their companies.

Bank of America
www.bankofamerica.com/smallbusiness/resourcecenter
> Online workshops, tools, and calculators to help you start, build,
> and manage your business.

Startup Nation
www.startupnation.com
> A community for entrepreneurs by entrepreneurs, Startup Nation
> was created to be a one-stop resource and boasts the largest
> online community of its kind in the world.

Visa Business Network on Facebook
http://usa.visa.com/business/
> Connect with small business owners, get expert advice, and
> reach the millions of potential customers on Facebook.

BLOGGERS

Brian Clark - Copy Blogger
www.copyblogger.com
> Copywriting tips for online marketing success.

Seth Godin
http://sethgodin.typepad.com/
> Seth writes the most popular marketing blog in the world,
> author of the bestselling marketing books of the last decade and
> founder of Squidoo.com, a fast-growing recommendation website.

Dianna Huff - Marcom Writer Blog
http://marcom-writer-blog.com/
> A B2B marcom expert delivers news and her own personal
> commentary on all things dealing with B2B marketing
> communications.

John Jantsch - Duct Tape Marketing
www.ducttapemarketing.com/blog
> Hands-on marketing ideas. John Jantsch's daily posts discuss
> what works – and what doesn't – when marketing a small business.

Guy Kawasaki - How to Change the World
http://blog.guykawasaki.com/
> Writing "A practical blog for impractical people," Guy Kawasaki
> remains one of the most popular business bloggers out there.
> A venture capitalist, Kawasaki 's blog remains a must-read
> for entrepreneurs.

Drew McLellan - Drew's Marketing Minute
www.drewsmarketingminute.com/
> With brief and to the point posts, Drew McLellan offers his marketing
> tips to help your business generate customer loyalty and sales.

BACK OFFICE SUPPORT

FedEx Office
www.fedexoffice.com
> The back office for small businesses and a branch office for medium to large businesses and mobile professionals.

MAGAZINE SOURCES

Forbes
www.forbes.com/entrepreneurs
> Advice, tips, and strategies from top experts for entrepreneurs.

Inc Magazine and Inc.com
www.inc.com
> Delivers advice, tools, and services to help business owners and CEOs start, run, and grow their businesses more successfully. Information and advice covers virtually every business and management task, including marketing, sales, finding capital, managing people, and more.

Smart Business Magazine and sbnonline.com
www.sbnonline.com
> A publisher of local management journals under the Smart Business name aimed at providing insight, advice, and strategy for executives of fast-growth, middle-market, and large companies. Publications are designed as concise packages that meet the information needs of decision-makers.

EMAIL SERVICE PROVIDERS

Get Response
www.getresponse.com

A Web-based email marketing software that delivers campaigns, offers, newsletters, follow-ups, and autoresponder messages.

iContact
www.icontact.com

An on-demand email marketing service that allows organizations of all sizes to easily create, send, and track email newsletters, RSS feeds, surveys, and autoresponders.

My Emma
www.myemma.com

A Web-based service that helps manage email marketing and communications from start to finish.

WEBSITE HOSTING AND DOMAIN REGISTRATION

Go Daddy
www.GoDaddy.com

The world's No. 1 ICANN-accredited domain name registrar for .COM, .NET, .ORG, .INFO, .BIZ and .US and dozens of other domain extensions.

ONLINE MEETING AND COLLABORATION SERVICES

GoToMeeting
www.gotomeetlng.com
> Offering Web-based remote access, support, and online meeting technologies.

ONLINE NETWORKING

LinkedIn
www.linkedin.com
> An online network of more than 20 million experienced professionals representing 150 industries from around the world. Helps keep you informed and puts you in touch with people and knowledge relevant to your business.

Slingshot
www.joinslingshot.com
> A online community that's part of a new national movement to create advocacy, awareness, and energy in support of small businesses, Slingshot is designed to connect and mobilize local small businesses.

SUPPORT ORGANIZATIONS

EO
www.eonetwork.org
> A global network of more than 6,600 business owners in 38 countries, EO enables entrepreneurs to learn and grow from each other, leading to greater business success and an enriched personal life.

SCORE "Counselors to America's Small Business"

www.Score.org

> Nonprofit association dedicated to educating entrepreneurs
> and the formation, growth, and success of small businesses
> nationwide.

Vistage

www.vistage.com

> Helps top executives and owners of small businesses take their
> careers—and their companies—to a higher level.

Index

surprise element, 13
suspects, 77, 79f12.1

T
target audience, 13, 63, 65, 67
target market
    banner advertising campaign, 95–96
    brochures, electronic or printed, 96–97
    case studies, 51–52
    competitive edge, 49
    Cookie Cutter Shop, 116
    defining, 44
    direct mail campaigns, 98–99
    event sponsorship, 100–101
    Five Key Questions, 13, 160
    identifying, 23, 43, 46–48
    lead referral campaigns, 99
    listing current/future, 50
    Marketing Machine™, 77–79, 79f12.1
    multiple, 45–46, 45f7.1
    multiple contacts with, 79, 79f12.1
    newsletters, client, 98
    no-risk offer, 126
    noise, removing the, 71
    pains of, 13
    pains of, identifying, 53
    public relations campaign, 100
    selection process, 48–49, 49 f7.2
    success leveraging, 46
    targeting, 45–46, 45f7.1
    worksheet, 48–49, 49f7.2, 50, 53f8.1
telemarketing campaign, 105–6
10-10-10 program, 106
three-step marketing, 20, 20f2.2
tool rental company, 59–60
trade magazine, 28
trade shows
    campaigns, 101–2
    marketing, 78, 97
    Marketing Machine™, 80
    marketing plan calendar, 134, 134f18.1, 136
    website listing, 129
transaction purchase, 142
trusted advisor, 74
TV ads, 9, 17–20, 78, 80, 100, 107
two-step marketing, 18, 18f2.1, 20, 20f2.2, 71

U
Upscale Business Meeting Space Provider, 97–98

V
van lettering, 54
video, 105, 126, 157
Vinyl Records Provider, 94

Reality Marketing
Revolution

Congratulations! You have made an important choice to join our revolution and rage against the old, broken marketing approach. Reality Marketing will set you free and help your business to thrive. To gain access to the secret archives and take advantage of resources not available to the general public, click on **www.realitymarketingrevolution/secrets.**

The team at Square2 Marketing is here to help you.

Square 2 Marketing helps...

- Business Owners
- Entrepreneurs
- Marketing Executives
- Corporate Marketing Managers
- Association Directors

Square 2 Marketing delivers...

- Improve performance of your marketing programs
- Improve performance of your sales teams
- Think out of the box, as to how you market your company
- Creatively make your company remarkable
- Train your people on how to think differently about your marketing approach

Square 2 Marketing is available to work with your organization to provide...

- Marketing Consulting
- Sales Consulting
- Marketing Workshops
- Speaking Engagements
- Educational Resources

Visit **www.square2marketing.com** and the work with do with clients to help them get their businesses to reach new heights.